The Pacific Insular Case of American Sāmoa

Line-Noue Memea Kruse

The Pacific Insular Case of American Sāmoa

Land Rights and Law in Unincorporated US Territories

palgrave
macmillan

Line-Noue Memea Kruse
Brigham Young University–Hawai'i
La'ie, Hawaii, USA

ISBN 978-3-319-88870-5 ISBN 978-3-319-69971-4 (eBook)
https://doi.org/10.1007/978-3-319-69971-4

Printed on acid-free paper

This Palgrave Macmillan imprint is published by Springer Nature
The registered company is Springer International Publishing AG
The registered company address is: Gewerbestrasse 11, 6330 Cham, Switzerland

This book is dedicated to my husband,
Vincent
For being the lighthouse

And

To my parents,
Joseph and Vernetta
Thank you for teaching me that perseverance is the hard work you do after you get tired of doing the hard work you already did

Preface

While in my doctorate studies, I came across an obscure supplemental article describing the changing land tenure in American Sāmoa. I felt the author was trying to convince me that communal lands are a significant problem for "progress" to take hold. From that article, my research, classes, and professional work I aligned to pursue the topics of individual land rights, communal land tenure, citizenship, and law. While I taught at the National University of Sāmoa, I conducted archival research on the alienation of land, while paying attention to societal and legal changes over time.

After moving from Sāmoa to American Sāmoa, I was hired to the post of Territorial Planner in the American Sāmoa Government, Department of Commerce. My professional responsibilities included strategic planning of the territory to advocate for safe, enjoyable, and orderly land use. As the first Sāmoan to hold this position in American Sāmoa, I felt the responsibility to ensure that the protections of the remaining communal lands are preserved for future Sāmoans to enjoy and use for the perpetuation of Sāmoan culture. If communal lands are eliminated or significantly reduced, the purpose and importance of the *fa'amātai* system may permanently fade away.

Lá'ie, HI

Line-Noue Memea Kruse

Acknowledgments

I would like to express my gratitude to the many people who saw me through this book; to all those who provided support, talked concepts out, read, wrote, offered comments, and assisted in the proofreading.

This research began as my doctorate thesis, minutes after my defense the entire committee remarked that this work should be published and after graduation I set out to do just that. This work is not only academic theory, this work is a culmination of passion, theory, boots on the ground professional and academic research, and my desire to write about issues that are sometimes difficult to discuss because of the emotions revolving around communal "native" land and Sāmoan culture. This work necessitated much conversation and dialogue which would be impossible to thank everyone. I want to express my heartfelt appreciation to my husband, Vincent, who supported and encouraged me despite all the time it took away from our family. To my children, Vaiausia, Tauavae, Fa'atoalia Michael, and Vaeolenofoafia Nicholas, for sharing mommy with her computer "business." To my parents, Joseph and Vernetta, for teaching me the value of a hard day's work and that nothing worthwhile comes without sacrifice. During the research and writing of this manuscript, the sacrifices you both made to stay with us in American Sāmoa for a year allowed me the time to finish writing. To my mother, Vernetta, the painter, creative writer, gardener, and the glue that binds our family, thank you for all the redlining and late-night conversations, draft after draft. To my in-laws Michael and Gail for their unwavering support and advice, your words of strength and encouragement are priceless. I must thank my siblings Ken, Teuila, and Keller for helping my family during life's journey without missing a beat to step in when I called upon you for help. Many thanks to Freddie and Tile, for being wonderful examples to the kids.

Without the support of American Sāmoa Government Department of Commerce director Keniseli F. Lafaele, I would not have been privileged to be part of the many planning and economic development projects in American Sāmoa or in the Pacific region, thank you for your trust. Fa'afetai tele lava to American Sāmoa Government Department of Commerce deputy director Uili Leauanae, a man with decades of service in government, village, and church but never mentions any of his accolades; thank you for your example and courage to fight the good fight.

A special note of thanks to American Sāmoa High Court Clerk Terry Fielding, who patiently retrieved cases and guided me through the resources I requested, some of which required great care because of the 2009 tsunami damage to select cases. At the American Samoa Government Department of Legal Affairs, Territorial Registrar's Office, I would like to thank Territorial Registrar Taito Sam White for permitting me to access *mātai* title records recorded since 1900. Also, I am grateful to Territorial Archivist James Himphill at the American Sāmoa Government Archives and Records for help in researching and locating archival records. I must also thank Territorial Librarian Justin Maga and Photo Curators Mary Tiumalu and Siata Siaosi at the Feleti Barstow Public Library for your time and assistance with archival research. At the National Archives at San Francisco, I would like to thank Archivist William Greene for assistance in locating specific records relating to the Naval era over American Sāmoa. Appreciation goes to Bernice Pauahi Bishop Museum Historian Desoto Brown for assistance in archival research.

I would like to thank Palgrave Macmillan Editors Michelle Chen and John Stegner for making this publication process feel easy going from start to finish.

Last and not least, I beg forgiveness of all those who have been with me over the course of the years and whose names I have failed to mention.

Contents

List of Figures

List of Tables

CHAPTER 1

Introduction

The February 19, 1900 General Order No. 540 of the US Naval Department was enacted vis-à-vis Executive Order No. 125-A, thus placing the "Sāmoan Group" under the control of the Naval Department.[1] The Naval Department had supreme legislative, executive, and judicial power over the Sāmoan Group (Gray 1960, p. 232).

The Naval Administration instituted American property laws alongside the traditional Sāmoan land tenure system in American Sāmoa. One of the significant property laws introduced was adverse land possession. Adverse land ownership rights were determined to be a milestone of enlightened western jurisprudence for land issues where Sāmoan customary laws were deemed insufficient, without merit, and uncivilized. The evolution of adverse land possession principles and rights in American Sāmoa has worked to erode the traditional communal land tenure system and *fa'asāmoa*[2] culture (customs and daily respectful behavior practiced by every Sāmoan) by laying the groundwork for individually owned land rights. Individually owned land classification is incongruent with the Sāmoan communal land tenure system. This book examines the early Naval Court decisions and the incorporation of adverse land possession rights that has evolved into the individually owned land classification in American Sāmoa.

The system of classifying land as individually owned takes away precious land holdings from communal tenure, which is not regulated or monitored by the American Sāmoa Government. Since the Naval Court decisions,

L.-N. Memea Kruse, *The Pacific Insular Case of American Sāmoa*,
https://doi.org/10.1007/978-3-319-69971-4_1

more and more lands have become individually owned, a trend that has damaged the communal land holding system and the *fa'asāmoa* culture. Preserving what remains of traditional land tenure cannot be achieved without examining the political and legal relationships between American Sāmoa and the United States. I examine these relationships to recommend practical alternatives to shelter Sāmoan cultural institutions within the American body-politic.

Cultural identity is the core basis of the Sāmoan people, and communally owned lands are the central foundation that will allow our cultural identity to survive in today's world. Communally owned lands provide a space for Sāmoans to live together with *āiga* (family, kin) members in a village setting to practice our Sāmoan traditions. The *fa'amātai* is the Sāmoan chiefly system and is fundamental to the sociopolitical organization of the Sāmoan society. It is the traditional system of governance. The *fa'amātai* system exists because there are communal lands for all members of the *āiga* to serve and protect the collective interests. The *fa'amātai* system is based on *āiga* clanship, composed of immediate *āiga* (father, brother, etc.) and a nexus of *āiga potopoto* (extended family). Every single *mātai* (chief) title has authority through which they exercise their oversight responsibilities over the *āiga*. The *mātai* has stewardship over the communal lands of their *āiga* and thus directs and supervises the *āiga* living on these land parcels according to tradition, cultural obligation, and duty.

Notes

1. Sāmoan Group—Convention Between the United States, Germany, and Great Britain to Adjust Amicably the Question Between the Three Governments in respect to the Sāmoan Group of Islands, December 2, 1899, 31 Stat. 1878, repr. in American Samoa Code Annotated (ASCA) sec. 5 (1973); Cession of Tutuila and Aunu'u, April 17, 1900, chiefs of Tutuila and Aunu'u Islands to US Government, repr. in ASCA sec. 2 (1981) [48 USC. § 1661]; Cession of Manu'a, July 14, 1904, King of Manu'a with chiefs of Manu'a Islands to US Government, repr. in ASCA sec. 2 (1981) [48 USC § 1661].
2. When dealing with *fa'asāmoa*, the main core values are taken from *gagana Sāmoa* as "*O tūma 'upu fa'aaloalo 'ia tausisi I ai ia faia I aso 'uma o le ōlaga o le Sāmoa*," translated in English as "Customs and ways of behaving as well as words of deference and respect which every Sāmoan must practise each day," S.P. Ma'ilo, *Palefuiono* (Apia: Fanuatanu, 1972). For additional resources of *fa'asāmoa*, see Tupua Tamasese, "Fa'aSāmoa speaks to my

heart and soul," (Keynote address to the Pasifika Medical Association Conference, Auckland, New Zealand, 2000); Asiata S. Va'ai, *Sāmoa Faamātai and the Rule of Law* (Apia: National University of Sāmoa, 1999); Malama Meleisea, *The Making of Modern Sāmoa: Traditional Authority and Colonial Administration in the History of Western Sāmoa* (Suva: Institute of Pacific Studies, 1987); Felix Keesing, *Modern Sāmoa: Its government and changing life* (London: George Allen & Unwin, 1934).

Reference

Gray, John A. 1960. *Amerika Sāmoa: A History of American Sāmoa and Its United States Naval Administration*. Annapolis: United States Naval Institute.

CHAPTER 2

Sāmoa and Traditional Land Tenure

Ia uluulu a mata-folau

American Sāmoa is in the Pacific Ocean and is the only US territory south of the equator, at 14 degrees south latitude and approximately 170 degrees west longitude. American Sāmoa is about 2300 miles south-southwest of Hawai'i, over 4100 miles southwest of San Francisco, and 1600 miles east-northeast of New Zealand. American Sāmoa consists of five volcanic islands and two atolls, called Rose Island and Swains Island. Tutuila, Aunu'u, Ofu, Olosega, and Ta'ū are the five main islands. The capital, Pago Pago, is located on the island of Tutuila, the most densely populated island that holds over 90 percent of the territory's residents. American Sāmoa's landmass is composed of 76 square miles; the island of Tutuila is the largest island with 56 square miles, while the remaining four islands are composed of 20 square miles.

American Sāmoa has a mountainous steep terrain and is in the path of the southeast trade winds, with an annual tropical rainfall that averages between 90 inches per year in the drier areas to 300 inches per year in the mountainous areas (2286 mm and 7620 mm) (National Park 2013, website). October to May is the rainy summer season (locals refer to it as the cyclone period), and the cooler, drier season occurs between June and September. American Sāmoa's topography is nearly two-thirds steep mountains covered in jungle. Thereby, most of the land is uninhabitable and inaccessible for agriculture cultivation, which intensifies the necessity

This Sāmoan phrase means to "have a vision while on a journey."

L.-N. Memea Kruse, *The Pacific Insular Case of American Sāmoa*,
https://doi.org/10.1007/978-3-319-69971-4_2

and urgency of protecting the habitable valley and flat plain lands. Cultivation of the mountainous slopes is impractical because of leaching and very thin soil, which will only support jungle vegetation. However, the soil in the valleys and plains is excellent for agriculture and human habitat. Land cannot be freely exchanged on the open market, as occurs in other market economies, and is considered essential to the preservation of the *fa'asāmoa* culture.

The Pago Pago harbor, a natural inlet in Tutuila on the central south coast, is one of the deepest and most sheltered harbors in the Pacific Ocean.[1] In the late 1800s, the United States had already established a diplomatic Consul office in the Independent State of Sāmoa (Sāmoa). During this time, the US Navy sought to construct naval and coaling stations in Tutuila, having recognized the significant military value of the harbor and its strategic positioning within the commercial shipping trade lines among East Asia, colonial-Pacific outposts, and the United States. The Pago Pago harbor was of great value for America as a naval station for coal and as a commercial transshipment outpost, especially during times of war, since Germany already had a presence in the Pacific region in Papua New Guinea, Solomon Islands, Bougainville Island, Nauru, Marshall Islands, Mariana Islands, Caroline Islands, and Sāmoa.

In 1900, separate negotiations were made by Tutuila and Aunu'u *mātai* (titled head of a Sāmoan extended family) with the United States. The islands of Tutuila and Aunu'u were politically organized as a sovereign kingdom apart from the Manu'a kingdom, which required separate and distinct negotiations from the reigning *mātai* leadership. In 1904, *mātai* of Manu'a Islands also signed the Deeds of Cession with the United States, thereby ceding the islands and atolls and their allegiance to the United States. US President William McKinley signed Executive Order 125-A, which authorized all ceded islands to be directly under the US Secretary of the Navy for a naval station (Title 48 U.S.C. §§ 1661, 1662). The Deeds of Cession were opposed by *mau* protestors against naval assimilation ordinances, arbitrary copra taxes, and their failure to respect Sāmoan lands and customs (Chappell 2000). Congressional ratification of the Deeds of Cession was not signed until 1929; perhaps the islands and region were considered testing grounds to determine its strategic need and importance. From 1900 to 1950, the US military had absolute control, power, and authority over the territory of American Sāmoa.

The dilemma of American expansion and colonial exploits was that the entanglements of cultures, traditions, races, foreign languages, and customs became a complex burden on American courts. During the American expansionist period into the Pacific and Atlantic Oceans during the nineteenth century, academics, politicians, legislators, and the military fought in a vicious national discourse over the issue of annexation of foreign lands and folding alien cultures into the American body-politic. Political and constitutional experts argued over how these foreign lands would be administered and what place, if any, they would have within the US political and legal system. American history books marginalize the place of American Sāmoa in the last years of the nineteenth century. Studies of empire shape the national consciousness, even outside academia, inspiring many people to consider the role empire has upon national identity and to examine the ways in which we see ourselves and those who are unlike ourselves (Hereniko and Wilson 1999).

Expansionist empire building in the Pacific faced constitutional challenges in how to absorb foreign island territories into the American body-politic. Three principal classifications addressed how territories would be absorbed into the United States. First, there could be states only, meaning that if the United States annexed any foreign possession, the possession would automatically become a state. This scenario pushed forward the idea that the only territories to be admitted into the United States were those that would automatically become states and any lands not fit for statehood would not be suitable as a territory.[2] Second, the United States could consist of states and territories. Territories would be indefinitely relegated to this political status and would not be given the same recognition and rights as states. Third, the United States could consist of states and territories dependent on congressional legislation and international treaties (Sparrow 2006, pp. 39–42). These three classifications were welcomed by the political elites, conservative jurists, and *papālagi*[3] (foreigner) businessmen (Gray 1960, pp. 3–5).

Fa'asāmoa and Communal Land Tenure

The significance of communal lands in American Sāmoa is rooted in the political structure of Sāmoan society. A Sāmoan proverb aptly describes Sāmoan clans: "*O Sāmoa ua taóto, a o se i'a mai moana, aua o le i'a a Sāmoa ua uma ona 'aisa.*" Translated into English it means, "Sāmoa is like an ocean fish divided into sections" (Meleisea 1987, p. 6). Communal lands and *mātai* titles are intertwined, without one or the other the *fa'asāmoa* system collapses.

Prior to the arrival of the *papālagi* in the 1800s, all land in American Sāmoa was considered "native" or in other words communally owned lands (Crocombe 1987, pp. 14–18). Communal lands were identified not by boundary markers or survey pegs, but as specific tracts of large, medium, and small lands collectively owned and controlled by the *āiga* (family) within a *nu'u* (village) and demarcated by settlement, cultivation, and virgin bush lands where the rivers and hills (natural features) were understood as boundary land markers (Meleisea 1987, pp. 1–6). However, uncultivated and unsettled lands belonged to the district, and negotiations for usage were exercised through the *nu'u*. The senior (highest) *mātai* title holders of a district had authority over all district lands (Meleisea 1987, p. 10). There are traditional *fa'asāmoa* cultural practices that allocate communal lands for specific purposes. For example, the *malae-fono* (meeting grounds) consist of uncultivated and unsettled parcels of land exclusively used as a central site for meetings of the principal *mātai* title holders of the village (Meleisea 1987, pp. 1–45). The *malae-fono* is considered a sacred place. *Malae-fono* sites in American Sāmoa have traditionally been prominent sites in the village. The number of such sites has diminished over the last 20 years due to natural disasters and the development of residential homes, roads, and church buildings.

The *mātai* system is particularly complex for foreigners to understand because it is not uncommon for *mātai* to hold more than one title from either the maternal or paternal lineage or even from the spouse's maternal or paternal lineage. In the traditional Sāmoan setting, *mātai* may also hold various titles within their own *āiga*. It is the *āiga* that bestows the chiefly titles upon the *mātai*. The *mātai*, once bestowed these chiefly titles by the *āiga*, exercise control over family communal lands and natural resources on these lands and command the decision-making process of the other family members (Holmes and Holmes 1992). The *mātai* are then responsible to their families for the overall welfare and stewardship of family lands. American Sāmoa still maintains this societal and cultural framework of *mātai* and communal land tenure.

Nu'u *(Village)*

A *nu'u* typically includes 200 and 500 people from multiple *āiga* groups in American Sāmoa.[4] There are two types of *āiga* groups within the context of Sāmoan culture: the immediate *āiga* and the *āiga potopoto* (extended kin). The immediate *āiga* is western society's version of the nuclear family and consists of parents and children. The *āiga potopoto* includes descendants from a common ancestor from either the maternal or paternal lines or both, as well as people related by marriage and adoption. In some cases, also included in *āiga potopoto* are extended family members from outside the *nu'u* who are brought into the domestic household to assist the *āiga*. In the twenty-first century, *āiga* members living overseas but still showing *tautua* (service) can still be considered *āiga potopoto* which permit them to lay claim to rights over and access to the *āiga* communal lands. However, without *tautua* to the *āiga* and *āiga potopoto*, there can be no justified execution of rights to the *āiga* communal lands by anyone. Traditional Sāmoan villages are patriarchal; sons typically live with their fathers, and daughters move to their husband's village. Malama Meleisea, cultural and legal history scholar from National University of Sāmoa, describes the political structure of the Sāmoan polity:

> Fishing, housebuilding (including felling and transporting timber), preparing feasts, hunting, clearing forests, and preparation of war, were among the many activities undertaken under the direction of the *fono*. *Mātai* worked along with untitled men and acted as work leaders; only the highest ranking *ali'i* were unlikely to take part in daily work. (Meleisea 1987, p. 7)

Mātai *(Chief)*

Within each *āiga* there was stratification: *mātai*, *'aumaga* (untitled men), and *'aualuma* (girls and women). Each of these stratified subgroups had its own dwelling units for specific duties and responsibilities under the *mātai* (Meleisea 1987). *'Aumaga* and *'aualuma* are distinct in terms of labor and status: the *'aumaga* are to serve as soldiers in war, fishermen, sportsmen, and cooks, and are responsible for beautifying the *āiga* lands (Meleisea 1987; Shaffer 2000, p. 48). *'Aualuma* serve as chaperones to the high-ranking individuals in the *āiga*, decorate guests' units, assist in preparations when *malaga* (visiting guests) come to the village, and perform other tasks given to them by the *mātai*. Prior to modernization, entire villages would interact by visiting each other, in a traditional social activity called *malaga*. Entire villages would travel to other villages for socialization and intervillage talks. The *mātai* would gather to discuss village matters, while the untitled men, women, and children from the host and guest villages would socialize.

American Sāmoan Fono *(Legislature)*

The American Sāmoa *Fono* under the Revised American Sāmoa Constitution is composed of traditional *matai*. The prerequisite to be an eligible Senator in the *Fono* is to be *mātai*, and the Senator must fulfill traditional duties and responsibilities to their registered constituency. Article II, § 3 (d) states Senators must "be the registered *mātai* of a Sāmoan family who fulfills his obligations as required by Sāmoan custom in the district from which he is elected" (Revised Constitution of American Sāmoa, art.II. § 3(d)). These obligations are not defined, and the High Court does not have delineated rules prescribing the precise method or custom that a village council must use to elect a Senator "in accordance with Sāmoan custom," because custom may vary in different counties. These local Constitutional provisions not only recognize the Sāmoan institution of *fa'amātai*, which establishes the chiefly title as the basis for eligibility to the Senate, but also allows for local custom to be practiced according to the will of the people in each district.

The *mātai* title holder is the leader within the *āiga* and the trustee of the communal land holdings of the family. *Mātai* is used synonymously to refer to an individual (both female and male) as a chief and a title holder. A *mātai* title holder can provide leadership to the *āiga* and can become a high *mātai* title holder if he or she gains a knowledge of *taeao* (history), oration with *taeao* mastery (role of the *tulafale mātai* title holder), knowledge of mythology and legends, genealogy lines, and the ability to recite proverbial expressions (Amerika Sāmoa Humanities Council 2009, p. 4). A person cannot be the chief of the *āiga* without a *mātai* title. The *mātai* distributes food, natural resources, and labor among the *āiga*. The hierarchical nature of the traditional Sāmoan polity means that all food, goods, shelter, and land are distributed and redistributed by this chiefly authority. The highest *mātai* distributes these assets accordingly and the lower *mātai* share their portions with the households within the *āiga* units. Ultimately, *fa'asāmoa* life for a Sāmoan is regulated by a set of laws and customs promulgated by village traditions, customs, and practices under the direction of the senior *mātai* of the village. No hard and fast rules can be generalized to every village in American Sāmoa, which is why *fa'asāmoa* has been able to survive modernization; it adapts to the changing lifestyle of its people. Table 2.1 depicts the traditional political structure of American Sāmoa, the districts, villages, and *Fa'asuaga* (paramount chief) who has ultimate leadership over its district and the village *mātais* within each district.

Table 2.1 American Sāmoan political structure

Districts	*Villages*	*Fa'asuaga*[a]
Sua	Masausi, Sailele, Masefau, Afono, Fagaitua, Amaua, Lauli'i	LE'IATO
Vaifanua	Vatia, Aoa, Onenoa, Tula, Alao	LE'IATO
Saole	Aunu'u, Utumea, Au'asi, Amouli, Alofau	FAUMUINA
Mao'putasi (Launiusaelua)	Aua, Leloaloa, Atu'u, Pago Pago, Fagatogo, Utulei, Gataivai, Faga'alu	MAUGA
Itū'au	Fagasa, Matu'u, Faganeanea, Nu'uuli	MAUGA
Fofō/Alataua	Leone/Asili, Amalu'ia, Afao, Atauloma, Nua, Seetaga, Agugulu, Fa'ilolo, Amanave, Poloa, Fagali'i, Malota, Fagamalo	TUITELE
Aitulagi/Leasina	A'asu, Aoloau, and half of Malaeloa	FUIMAONO
Tūalātai	Vailoatai, Taputimu, Futiga, and half of Malaeloa	SATELE
Tūalāuta	Vaitogi, Ili'ili, Pavaia'i, Faleniu, Tafuna	LETULI
Manu'a	Ofu, Olosega, Sili, Ta'ū, Fitiuta, Faleasao	TUI MANU'A

Amerika Sāmoa Humanities Council (2009, p. 63)

[a]*Fa'asuaga* is defined as a paramount chief in *American* Sāmoa

Figure 2.1 depicts the political districts of Tutuila and Manu'a where the abovementioned villages and paramount *mātai* title holders had *pule* (authority) and control over the lands during the 1800s.

Prior to the introduction of plantation-cash cropping by the US Navy, *āiga* clans worked together by planting and harvesting crops, protecting farm lands, and shielding the village from outsiders.[5] *Taro* is the most important staple crop in American Sāmoa. Tutuila utilizes the dry-land method of cultivation while Aunu'u Island and some farms in the Manu'a islands use the wet-land method. There are over 20 local varieties, including *Niue*, *Manu'a*, *Pa'epa'e*, *Pula Sama*, *Fa'ele'ele*, and *Tusi* (Brooks and Utifiti 2001). *Taro* is interplanted in large and small areas in between *ta'amū* (variety of giant taro), banana mats, coconut, *ulu* (breadfruit) trees, or in bush lands. Due to the immense rainfall and the fact that most of the islands are composed of vertical uninhabitable slopes, preparation for planting and harvesting has historically required a collective effort to ensure there was enough food to feed everyone in the village. Sāmoans do not cultivate *taro* through tilling but rather by using the *oso*, a planting stick, and weeds as mulch. Bush (virgin) lands have unique importance because of their potential use as rotational grounds for agriculture cultivation. The

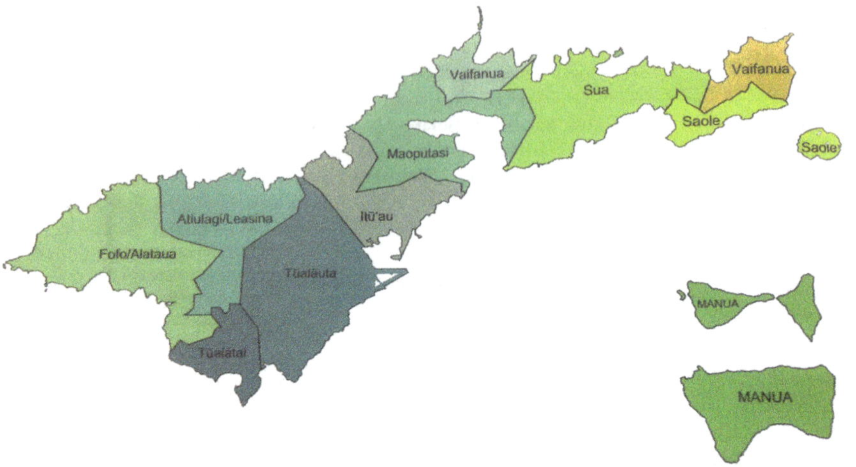

Fig. 2.1 Traditional districts in American Sāmoa Amerika Sāmoa Humanities Council (2009, p. 52)

soil rehabilitates itself from crops rotated throughout the year and provides ecosystem services such as food, wood, fertilizer, water, and medicinal resources, as well as cultural benefits of recreational and spiritual spaces. Prior to western medicine, the cultural and medicinal resources found in the bush lands were highly important for treating and curing ailments. Additionally, the bush lands are of great importance for cultural formalities of sharing and gifting wood and food to extended *āiga* clans from visiting villages and counties. Although American Sāmoa now practices subsistence farming and cash cropping, bush lands are still vital to food security and the practice of cultural traditions because of the communal lifestyle under the *fa'asāmoa*. According to the most recent agricultural census in 2008 by the US Department of Agriculture National Agriculture Statistics Service (USDA NSAA), 19,003 acres of cropland in American Sāmoa are used for farming (US Department of Agriculture 2008, Part 55).[6] The total use of cropland represents approximately 30 percent of all land area in American Sāmoa (American Samoa Statistical Yearbook 2013, p. 174). These cultivated croplands are not identified in the registered land tenure classifications, so presumably they are unregistered bush lands that are maintained under the communal land system. The preservation of the bush-croplands is significant, as it will protect cultivation and lands for a growing future population. These lands also represent income to families and provide food security for *āiga* clans that depend on these bush lands for agricultural consumption at home.

The power and authority within the *fa'amātai* cannot be overstated. The *mātai* title holder grants resources, responsibilities, access to and use of all *āiga* communal lands. If there are agricultural crops or river fish on different parts of village lands under two or three *mātais*, each *āiga* group must go through their individual *mātai* to ask for permission to access and use these different communal lands and their resources from each *mātai* title holder. There are also temporary and permanent land restrictions that a *mātai* can initiate for land parcels under his supervision. The *mātai* title holder can place *sā* (taboo) on agricultural staples during times of famine to ensure ample food and resources when a *malaga* visits. This power means food and land is restricted, based on the will of the *mātai*. The *mātai* titles and the specific lands that relate to them are controlled by the *āiga* and *āiga potopoto*, all operating under the senior *mātai* title holder. This senior *mātai* title holder is elected by consensus of high *mātai* title holders. Consensus is the primary decision-making method. Unlike in some Melanesian cultures, in traditional Sāmoan culture there is no overarching tribunal of Sāmoan *mātai* title holders over all *mātai* title holders throughout the Sāmoan archipelago. Formidable village alliances have historically been forged during times of war, but these are temporary and designed for mutual self-preservation.

There are two types of *mātai* titles: *ali'i* and *tulāfale*. Meleisea describes these *mātai* titles as follows:

> *Ali'i* titles were those which traced sacred origins through genealogies which begin with Tagaloa-a-lagi, the creator, and are linked to major aristocratic lineages. *Tulāfale* had more utilitarian associations, in accordance with their role of rendering service to and oratory on behalf of the *ali'i*. (Meleisea 1987, p. 8)

The traditional *fa'amātai* system is a complex configuration of *mātai* titles, all ordered relative to each other. *Mātai* titles are based upon kinship relations, mythology, and genealogical history but also upon one's ability to garner loyalty and support within the *āiga* and *āiga potopoto* structure. Each nuclear household has a *mātai* title holder in traditional Sāmoan society and on communal lands within the village. Within the village, there is a hierarchy of *mātai* title holders. Each *mātai* title is ranked relative to the others and is, in the sense of the English language, "owned" by the *āiga*. *Suli moni*, *suli si'i*, and *suli fa'i* are distinctions within the traditional Sāmoan *fa'amātai* system. *Suli moni* is a blood descendant. *Suli si'i* is someone from a different family who has lived and rendered service to the *Sa'o*.[7] *Suli fa'i* is the adopted heir that is not blood kin but an adopted child or a daughter's husband that lives with the *āiga* and also renders *tautua* to the *Sa'o* (Crocombe 1987, pp. 75–79). These distinctions are important to a Land and Titles case when there is a disputed *mātai* title; families can petition the court to differentiate among the three to determine the strongest claim to the *mātai* title.[8]

The *mātai pule* is limited by the responsibility to care for the *āiga* and extended *āiga*. If the *mātai* acts in a way that the *āiga* feels is unbecoming, or if the *mātai* does not take good care of the *āiga*, the *āiga* may remove the *mātai* title from the individual and thus remove his authority over the family lands. Pacific Islands Studies expert Ron Crocombe and former director of the Institute of Pacific Studies at the University of South Pacific outlines the nexus between *āiga* and *fa'amātai* systems in relation to communal land tenure features:

1. Land is owned by extended family *aiga*, which take their names from their respective *mātai* titles.
2. Control over land is gained indirectly by acquiring the specific title which has *pule* over the land.
3. Access to the title itself is gained primarily by descent from a previous title holder or occasionally by exceptional service to the present title holder, rather than by descent from those actually occupying the land. (Crocombe 1987, p. 78)

In American Sāmoa, unlike Sāmoa, there are three significant differences in the *fa'amātai* system. First, there exists a *mātai* title registry administered by the Government. Second, only *mātai* titles that were registered before the cutoff date of January 1, 1969 are recognized. Third, only one person may be assigned to each *mātai* title (A.S.C.A. § 1.0401 et seq., 1968). In American Sāmoa, the law even makes it a criminal act for an individual to use an unregistered *mātai* title (A.S.C.A. § 1.0401 (1968), § 1.0402 (1977), § 1.0403 (1981), §1.0404 (1981); *Toilolo v. Poti*, 23 A.S.R.2d 130 (1993)). If a *mātai* title recognized by the *āiga* was not registered before the cutoff date of for a *mātai* title). This bill seeks to address the inequality of gender-based favoring of male descendants, limiting the right to *mātai* title to bloodline and endorsement of family.

9. Original empirical research of all registered *mātai* titles in the Office of the Territorial Registrar between January 2, 1969 and 2013. *Mātai* titles were tabulated based upon the Office of the Territorial Registrar's determination as a registered *mātai* title in situations of death, resignation, or high court cases (Meeting with Territorial Registrar, October 10, 2014).
10. Western Sāmoa (prior to sovereign independence) Chief Justice Marsack and President of the Land and Titles Court stated that the *pule* rests with the successor in title not to heirs of body.
11. See Chap. 2.
12. The first Chief Justice in Sāmoa under the Treaty of Berlin was a Swedish citizen.

References

2007 Census of Agriculture. American Samoa (2008)—Territory, District, and County Data. US Department of Agriculture, v. 1, Part 55, AC-07-55. June 2011.

American Sāmoa Code Annotated (A.S.C.A.) § 1.0401 et seq. 1968.

American Sāmoa Government Department of Commerce. *Statistical Yearbook* 2013. Published Annually. http://www.doc.as.gov.

Amerika Sāmoa Humanities Council. 2009. *A History of American Sāmoa*. Honolulu: Bess Press.

Brooks, Fred, and Makeati Utifiti. 2001. *Crop Profile in American Samoa*. Working Paper, American Samoa Community College, American Sāmoa.

Campbell, Ian C. 1989. *A History of the Pacific Islands*. Berkeley: University of California Press.

Chappell, David. 2000. "The Forgotten Mau: Anti-Navy Protest in American Samoa, 1920–1935." *Pacific Historical Review* 69 (2): 217–260.

Crocombe, Ron. 1987. *Land Tenure in the Pacific*. 3rd ed. Suva: University of South Pacific.

Gray, John A. 1960. *Amerika Sāmoa: A History of American Sāmoa and Its United States Naval Administration*. Annapolis: United States Naval Institute.

Hart, John W., et al. 1971. *History of Sāmoa*. Apia: Church Schools of Western Sāmoa.

Henry, Brother Fred. 1980. *Sāmoa: An Early History*. Pago Pago: American Sāmoa Department of Education.

Hereniko, Vilisoni, and Rob Wilson, eds. 1999. *Inside Out: Literature, Cultural Politics, and Identity in the New Pacific*. Lanham: Rowman & Littlefield Publishing.

Holmes, Lowell D., and Ellen Rhoads Holmes. 1992. *Sāmoan Village Then and Now*. Fort Worth: Harcourt Brace Jovanovich College Publishers.
Krämer, Augustin. 1994. *The Samoa Islands*. Vol. I. Auckland: Pasifika Press.
Leibowitz, Arnold H. 1989. *Defining Status: A Comprehensive Analysis of United States Territorial Relations*. Norwell: Martinus Nijhoff.
Marsack, C.C. 1958. *Notes on the Practice of the Court and Principles Adopted in Hearing of Cases Affecting (1) Samoan Mātai Titles; and (2) Land Held According to Customs and Usages of Western Samoa*. Apia: Land and Titles Court.
Meleisea, Malama. 1987. *The Making of Modern Samoa: Traditional Authority and Colonial Administration in the Modern History of Western Samoa*. Suva: Institute of the South Pacific.
Merry, Sally E. 2000. *Colonizing Hawai'i: The Cultural Power of Law*. Princeton: Princeton University Press.
National Park of American Sāmoa, National Park Service Website. 2013 Continually Updated. https://www.nps.gov/npsa/index.htm. Accessed 5 February 2013.
Pearl, Frederic B., and Sandy Loiseau-Vonruff. 2007. "Father Julien Vidal and the Social Transformation of a Small Polynesian Village (1787–1930): Historical Archaeology at Massacre Bay, American Samoa." *International Journal of Historical Archaeology* 11 (1): 32–59.
Revised Constitution of *American* Sāmoa, art. II, § 3(d).
Shaffer, Robert. 2000. *American Sāmoa: 100 Years Under the United States Flag*. Honolulu: Island Heritage Publications.
Sparrow, Bartholomew H. 2006. *The Insular Cases and the Emergency of American Empire*. Lawrence: University Press of Kansas.
Title 48 U.S.C. §§1661, 1662.
Toilolo v. Poti, 23 A.S.R. 2d 130 1993.

CHAPTER 3

American International Expansion

In the late eighteenth century, the American Continental Congress laid the groundwork for acquiring land "possessions" by annexing "crown lands" west of the Alleghenies and beyond the Ohio River to the royal province of Quebec (Adams 1896–1904, pp. xii–xiii; Sato 1886, pp. 192–193). The colonies felt that the possession of these lands, later established as "The Northwest," was crucial to connecting and unifying the entire soon-to-be confederacy and allowing for the economic expansion of current and future member states. The federal government created the Northwest Ordinance of 1787 to establish the government of the Northwest Territory. The Ordinance specified that these new areas were to be organized into territories and then, in whole or in part, admitted as states (Leibowitz 1989, p. 6; Sparrow 2006, pp. 14–20). The Northwest Territory (which was already being settled by immigrants from the original states at the time of the Constitution's drafting in 1787) was the first "territory" of the United States.

The Northwest Territory became the common property of the United States, fulfilling the desire of the colonists to further the expansion and collective power of the confederation (Adams 1896–1904, p. 43). The lands under the Northwest Territory included lands east of the Mississippi between the Ohio River and Great Lakes, which later became the states of Ohio, Indiana, Illinois, Michigan, and Wisconsin. The early conquests of land emboldened the newly established Continental Congress to consolidate their power and control over these early territorial lands.

L.-N. Memea Kruse, *The Pacific Insular Case of American Sāmoa*,
https://doi.org/10.1007/978-3-319-69971-4_3

To enable and encourage the settling of the territory by *papālagi* Americans, native American people were systematically removed from their homelands and moved to foreign lands (from the perspective of indigenous tribes, any lands not connected to their tribal lands were foreign) without adequate infrastructure, water, or food, subjugated to Americanization projects, Christianized, and forced to learn and speak English. Native Americans resisted the brutal and imperialistic actions of "benevolent assimilation" despite the claims that these acts were committed to promote integration, democracy, and freedom. Indigenous native American tribes rebelled. Nobel Memorial Prize Economist Gunnar Myrdal wrote the "disconnect between American egalitarian ideals and the reality of America's practices" manifested itself as native American defiance against Americanization projects and their forced removal from homelands by armed military (Román 2006, pp. xi–xii).

Anthropologist and ethnographer Patrick Wolfe, whose work has trail blazed settler-colonialism studies, addresses race as much more than simply a social construct within settler colonialism. Wolfe asserts that racism is but a targeting process and that the primary motive for elimination is not race or religion, ethnicity, or grade of civilization. The true motive is access to territory. He further argued that "land acquisition as well as the wealth and opportunities it brought were the principal factors that motivated settlement and imposed the interminable process of Indigenous dispossession, elimination by various means, and the legitimation of settler sovereignty over both land and people" (Wolfe 2006, p. 388). Wolfe suggests the logic of elimination in settler colonialism strives to tear apart an indigenous society to form a colonial society on land stolen from the native people (Wolfe 2006). This logic of elimination specifically produces the "breaking-down of native title into alienable individual freeholds." Additionally, elimination supports the colonial subversion of animate native citizenship through religious conversion and resocialization in residential schools where only English is allowed—the fulfillment of biocultural assimilation (Lemkin 1944, p. 79). Removing the younger generations from the older generations incrementally breaks down the transference of oral history, shared value systems of indigenous traditions, culture, and language.

However, it is worth noting that in this discourse of foreign lands being annexed into the US political system, race presented a foundational bias upon the perceived political responsibility to protect American culture and civility from foreign cultures and their traditions. In the late nineteenth century, the United States fashioned a blueprint for nation-building in the Pacific to counter Europe's system of imperialism. US colonial structures were described as benevolent and compared to Spain's cruel subjugation and domination helped to garner public and political support (Kaplan 1994, pp. 3–19). Nationalists were fearful that with the American flag spreading to distant lands and "savage" races, protectionist policies were needed to prevent any heathen practices from entering American society. Claiming to protect American culture from the perceived inferior races were prominent figures including Henry Cabot Lodge, Theodore Roosevelt, Reginald Horsman, Carl Schurz, Simeon Baldwin, Sir Walter Scott, and John W. Burgess—all of whom espoused the idea of "Teutonic" superiority over the uncivilized races of dissimilar island people (Kaplan 1994, pp. 3–19). The tone of national politics was very exclusionary; Melville Fuller's Supreme Court in 1896 passed the "separate but equal doctrine" implanting segregation and inequality in *Plessy v. Ferguson*. The Constitution's almost total silence on territorial expansion gave conservatives, military hawks, and Teutonic (or otherwise Anglo-Saxon) campaigners free reign to determine how territorial foreigners would be treated by the United States and who might be considered as such.

American expansionism during the early twentieth century moved quickly from the looming guerilla wars over the Philippines to the assertion of American political rights in Cuba and Puerto Rico. The United States savored its newfound identity as a superpower country, sending US Navy convoys overseas to establish military bases around the world and to solidify its colonial posts. With these newly acquired lands came foreign people and dissimilar cultures, languages, customs, and traditions.

Early land acquisition experiments in power, control, hegemony, and conquest—all in the interest to fulfilling the American ideal of democracy and freedom—became the blueprint for spreading American ideology and its expansionist propaganda. The 1840s era of Manifest Destiny was coupled with 1859 Darwinist theory to fuel American attempts to stretch its empire across the seas and into other parts of the world (Kaplan 2002, pp. 95–96). The United States embraced its role as an imperial giant when Spain ceded Puerto Rico, Guam, and the Philippines in 1898 to America as spoils of the Spanish-American War. The United States annexed Hawai'i through the 1898 Congressional Newlands Resolution, despite massive Hawai'ian protests against the Annexation treaty (Silva 2004). This resolution failed to pass in Congress; however, the annexation of Hawai'i still proceeded unabated. These American-colonial outposts were governed under the territorial structure laid out 111 years earlier by the Northwest Ordinance.

Early US Interest in Sāmoa

The US Government started to receive reports from sailors, seamen, and missionaries about migration to the "Great South Sea" and the bustling commercial trading and whaling activities. In 1839, the Department of Navy sent four ships, the *Vincennes*, the *Porpoise*, the *Peacock*, and the *Flyfish* to complete five weeks of scientific and navigational research in the Sāmoa Group. The ships moored in Upolu, Savai'i, and Tutuila. They collected information and data on land and water measurements, as well as astronomical and meteorological data in American Sāmoa (Amerika Samoa Humanities Council 2009, pp. 24–25). US Commodore Charles Wilkes, who was the highest authority in the US Government in the Sāmoa Group at that time, led this military expedition and determined that the US citizens trading in the Sāmoa Group required an official American presence for security. Without authorization or notification of the Department of State, Congress, or the President, Wilkes appointed John Williams Jr. to be the first US consul in Sāmoa.[1] Since Wilkes initiated this appointment without proper authority, however, Williams was relegated to being a commercial agent with no diplomatic powers for eight years.

In 1871, New Yorker W.H. Webb and his steamship company were contracted to transport coal by steamship between San Francisco and the South Pacific. Webb contracted US Navy Captain E. Wakeman to determine whether the Pago Pago harbor could be a suitable coaling station for coal-burning steamships. Wakeman reported to the US Navy that Germany was vying for all of Sāmoa and that, without US intervention, the islands would become German outposts under the Kaiser.

On February 14, 1872, US Navy Commander Richard Meade was officially sent on behalf of the Department of State to determine the feasibility of a US Naval Station in Pago Pago (Amerika Samoa Humanities Council 2009, pp. 24–25). Meade surveyed the Pago Pago harbor and the submerged reef in the bay area and set out to initiate relationships with the paramount chiefs to pave the way for an expanded American presence. Meade negotiated the Meade-Mauga Treaty with Paramount Chief Mauga and the *mātai* of the eastern side for the use of the harbor and the establishment of a board to oversee regulations in exchange for friendship and protection from the United States (Amerika Samoa Humanities Council

2009, pp. 28–29). Unbeknownst to Paramount Chief Mauga, who had full authority and powers to enter into the Meade-Mauga Treaty on behalf of his people, the US Senate never ratified this document. Paramount Chief Mauga did not know that the signed Meade-Mauga Treaty was still subject to the ratification by US Congress. Ironically, Meade, who did not have the full authority himself to execute a bi-lateral treaty on behalf of the United States, doubted whether Mauga had the authority to sign the treaty on behalf of his people. Wilkes also hid from Williams the fact that he had no authority or powers to appoint foreign diplomats on behalf of the US Department of State.

While Wilkes was conducting unauthorized military missions in the Sāmoan Islands, US military personnel in Hawai'i also made advances into the Sāmoan Islands without congressional approval or presidential proclamations. The US Pacific Fleet Admiral and US Minister Resident in Honolulu sent instructions to Commander Richard W. Meade to promote "by all legal and proper means, American interests and enterprises," which Meade faithfully initiated after his arrival in Pago Pago on February 14, 1872 (Amerika Samoa Humanities Council 2009, pp. 60–61). Meade, fulfilling these instructions, drafted an agreement entitled "Commercial Regulations, etc." with Mauga. The agreement stipulated that in exchange for the exclusive "privilege" of establishing a naval station in Pago Pago harbor (only Tutuila was discussed, not Manu'a or Aunu'u Islands), the United States promised to protect the people of Pago Pago (US Congress 1875, pp. 6–7). US President Grant pushed forth this agreement to the US Congress; however, the US Congress never ratified it because it was thought to be against US national foreign policy.

These early stages of negotiations between the US military personnel and the high chiefs of Pago Pago marked the beginning of the American paternalistic attitude toward the illiterate Sāmoan chiefs. The US Foreign Relations Committee, to which this treaty was assigned, immediately tabled it; the Committee was focused on reconstruction efforts at home and turned a blind eye to the military's exploits in the Sāmoan islands (US Congress 1875, pp. 6–7).

President McKinley's approach to the Anglo-German negotiations over Sāmoa was basically to abstain; he deferred to the Navy and its determination was to hold the Tutuila harbor and its coal shed operations for trans-Pacific trade (McKinley 1938, pp. 221–228). McKinley believed that the Berlin Agreement guaranteed US treaty rights to Tutuila. British and German rights in Tutuila would be canceled together with American rights in Upolu and Savai'i (Western Sāmoa) (National Archives 1898). In 1889, the Berlin Treaty was ratified by the United States, Great Britain, and Germany "to adjust amicably the questions which have arisen between them in respect to the Sāmoan group of Islands, as well as to avoid all future misunderstanding in respect to their joint or several rights and claims of possession or jurisdiction therein" (Treaty of Berlin, art.I). US Secretary of State John Hay believed that Tutuila was "the most important island in the Pacific as regards harbor conveniences for our navy, and a station on the trans-Pacific route" (Hay 1899). The Tripartite Convention of 1899 balkanized the Sāmoa Islands; the United States accepted the eastern Sāmoan Islands of Tutuila, Aunu'u, and Manu'a, while all the rest of Sāmoa fell to Great Britain (Gray 1960, p. 101). In exchange, Great Britain ceded rights to Germany for Tonga, Solomon Islands, and West Africa, thus fortifying British economic interests in Southern Africa (Gray 1960, pp. 101–102).

The US Congress sought to stake claim to the Pacific Islands through legislation and military force to propel the United States itself onto the international stage. For example, the Guano Islands Act of 1856 authorized any US citizen finding guano deposits to take possession of islands not occupied or under another government, effectively making all indigenous inhabitants invisible under this commercial expansionist scheme (Guano Islands Act, 11 Stat.119).[2] Great Britain cornered the South American market for guano resources with their colonial outposts. In response, the US Congress granted the authority for American traders to essentially claim ownership of lands and natural resources based on guano findings. Approximately 60 islands, including the Pacific Islands of Howland, Baker, and Jarvis, were dispossessed from indigenous populations through the Guano Islands Act.

US Naval Commandant Alfred Mahan campaigned for the establishment of US Naval bases in the Pacific to support and protect expanding commercial and military efforts (Stayman 2009, p. 5; US GAO 1997, p. 9). The expansion of US Naval bases created a buffer zone to protect the western continental shores and seemed to be a good strategy for securing the trans-Pacific trade routes. American expansion into Pago Pago was accomplished not through legislative, executive, congressional, or military design but rather by a few interested individuals determined to control the island, the harbor, and the trans-Pacific trade route. As the Sāmoan civil wars continued, several Americans of the Central Polynesian Land and Commercial Company (CPLCC) bartered and bought 414 square miles—approximately 300,000 acres of land—from the *mātai* of Tutuila, Upolu, Manono, and Savai'i (Gilson 1970, pp. 280–288; Masterman 1934, pp. 106–113). The CPLCC were notoriously manipulative land agents from San Francisco and Hawai'i who persuaded Sāmoans to trade or sell tracts of communal lands in return for weapons and ammunition at nominal fees (Tansill 1940, p. 9; Masterman 1934, p. 116; Gilson 1970, pp. 282–283). The CPLCC transactions in Sāmoa were dubious at best, "the documents in question described the land in the crudest fashion, stated no total or unit price to be paid for it, required by way of immediate payment only nominal deposits pending the outcome of surveys, and stipulated no time limit on the company's right or obligation to complete the surveys or its purchases" (Gilson 1970, p. 284).

In 1872, Captain Meade arranged for shipping rights in Pago Pago harbor while US President Grant sent Colonel Albert Steinberger as Special Commissioner to Sāmoa—even though Steinberger also held economic interests in the CPLCC. President Grant hoped that the Steinberger report on the island's economic potential would persuade the US Foreign Relations Committee to reassess the Meade-Mauga Treaty, but the treaty never made it out of committee for a full Congressional vote. The CPLCC hoped to gain favor with Steinberger by pushing hard for the US acquisition of Pago Pago so they could sell their bartered or cheaply bought tracts of land to the US government (Gilson 1970, pp. 291–305). American businessmen held 300,000 acres of land through various schemes and manipulative negotiations across the Sāmoa archipelago; these lands were alienated from Sāmoan customary landholdings. While American businessmen were swallowing up large tracts of land, the American military was scheming to enlarge their footprint in Pago Pago because of its harbor. All the while, Sāmoan clans were engaged in civil war, unaware of the geopolitical hostilities raging around them.

Sāmoa Islands Politicking

In 1875, after many wars and deaths, the high chiefs decided by consensus to establish the "Kingship," or rule for four-year periods, with the throne rotating between the houses of Malietoa and Tupua. The *Ta'imua* (House of High Chiefs) was composed of 15 members who were openly nominated and approved by the sitting "king." This house had an advisory board and helped the "king" with drafting legislation and regulation of laws. The *Faipule* (Lower House) had a membership of one representative, elected by district ballots, for every 2000 individuals (Ryden 1933, pp. 274–275, 291). No law could be passed without the approval of the majority of representatives. This newly established government vested power and authority in the legislature (*Ta'imua* and *Faipule*) rather than the throne, demonstrating how democracy and its forming value system was taking root within the Sāmoa Islands (Ryden 1933, pp. 200–308).

Germany, America, and Great Britain aligned themselves with various sitting kings and advanced their interests through these figureheads. All the while, these kings took advantage of these foreign governments, utilizing their skills of artful prose and politicking with different governments requesting protection against other foreign countries and internal. German Chancellor Bismarck wanted to simply annex the Sāmoa archipelago and impose martial law to quell High Chief Mata'afa and his attempts to solidify Sāmoan interests against foreigners. Bismarck also wanted to silence American and British critics of German policies in the Sāmoa Islands by assuming full authority and supreme control of the islands (Tansill 1940, p. 108).

In March 1889, American, British, and German naval ships were moored in Apia harbor on the island of Upolu, ready for outright war over exclusive rights to Pago Pago harbor (on Tutuila Island) and the Southern Ocean trans-Pacific trade route. A two-day hurricane hit the Sāmoa Islands, capsizing ships and causing many deaths and serious injuries in its wake (Gray 1960, pp. 88–91). The hurricane's destruction of all military vessels resulted in a cessation of hostilities between America, Great Britain, and Germany.

Condominium, No Sāmoan Representation

The three major foreign powers in the Sāmoan archipelago were also aware of the internal tension among the warring Sāmoan factions. A key conflict among Malietoa Tanumafili I, Tupua Tamasese, and To'oa Malietoa Mata'afa Iosefo centered on the question of who would be the new king after the 1898 passing of Malietoa Laupepa from typhoid fever. When Mata'afa's men around Apia attacked and killed British and American military men in retaliation for the destruction of Sāmoan homes by Anglo-American bombardment, it led to direct intervention in the form of an international conference over the Pacific holdings. The Americans wanted to secure the Pago Pago harbor, Germans wanted to protect their large plantations in Upolu and Savai'i, and the British wanted to retain Tonga and their other international outposts. The entire convention on the "Sāmoan problem" proceeded without Sāmoan participation.

The drawn-out conflict among Germany, America, and Great Britain, coupled with the dreadful hurricanes in the Sāmoa Islands, compelled the major powers to negotiate the Tripartite Convention (the Berlin Conference) on April 29, 1899; it was ultimately ratified in 1900 by the US Congress. The parties present included the president of the United States, the emperor of Germany, the king of Prussia, the queen of the United Kingdom and Ireland, and the empress of India and British representative. The Berlin Conference recognized Malietoa Laupepa as the King of Sāmoa and believed that his signature attested to a certificate that would establish the assent of Sāmoa to the Treaty of Berlin (Treaty of Berlin 1889, art. VIII, sec. 2; 26 Stat. 1497). Conspicuously, there were no Sāmoan representatives at this Conference, even though the Sāmoan "kings" and high chiefs had worked for years with government and military officials to develop bi-lateral working relationships. Although it was completed without the participation of the sitting King Malietoa Tanumafili I (son of Malietoa Laupepa) or any representative of the *Ta'imua* or *Faipule*, the Berlin Treaty claimed to be "promoting as far as possible the peaceful and orderly civilization of the people of these Islands" (Treaty of Berlin 1889, art. VIII, sec. 2; 26 Stat. 1497). The transparency of this thinly disguised attempt to protect each signatory country's economic and naval interest is especially apparent in Article III. The body of the treaty is relatively brief:

> Article I
>
> The General Act concluded and signed by the aforesaid Powers at Berlin on the 14th day of June, A.D. 1889, and all previous treaties, conventions and agreements relating to Sāmoa, are annulled.
>
> Article II
>
> Germany renounces in favor of the United States of America all her rights and claims over and in respect to the Islands of Tutuila and all other islands of the Sāmoan group east of Longitude 171 degrees west of Greenwich.
>
> Great Britain in like manner renounces in favor of the United States of America all her rights and claims over and in respect to the Island of Tutuila and all other islands of the Sāmoan group east of Longitude 171 degrees west of Greenwich.
>
> Reciprocally, the United States of America renounces in favor of Germany all her rights and claims over and in respect to the Islands of Upolu and

Savai'i and all other Islands of the Sāmoan group west of Longitude 171 degrees west of Greenwich.

Article III

It is understood and agreed that each of the three signatory Powers shall continue to enjoy, in respect to their commerce and commercial vessels, in all the islands of the Sāmoan group, privileges and conditions equal to those enjoyed by the sovereign Powers, in all ports which may be open to the commerce of either of them. (Faleomavaega 2014, website)

In return for Great Britain's renunciation of all rights and interests in Sāmoa, Germany ceded all its rights in Solomon Islands, Tonga, Bougainville, West Africa, and Zanzibar to Great Britain (Ryden 1933, pp. 568–572). Great Britain and America combined forces to suppress Mata'afa's efforts to consolidate Sāmoan resistance to all foreigners. At the same time, Great Britain and the United States were also working to obstruct Germany's influence in the Pacific region under Kaiser Wilhelm II. Their growing distrust of "Kaiserism" and Germany's naval and colonial expansions facilitated the ease with which American forces joined Great Britain in 1917 to destroy Germany and the Kaiser in World War I (Balfour 1964).

1900 and 1904 Deeds of Cession

Whaling in the South Pacific during the 1800s was considered a glorious and highly prosperous adventure. The United States had multiple whaling ships operating in the South Pacific, most notably outside the Northwestern Hawai'ian isles. US Commander Richard W. Meade, Jr., Commander of the US Navy vessel *Narrangansett*, entered into an agreement called "Commercial Regulations, etc." with Mauga that granted sole rights to access and use of the Pago Pago harbor (Sunia 1988). The Commercial Regulations were never binding because they never won approval by the President or ratification by the US Congress, but they nevertheless promoted the commercial relationship between the US and American Sāmoa.

The Treaty of Friendship and Commerce of 1878 and the General Act of 1889 further strengthened the relationship (Faleomavaega 2014, website). The 1878 Treaty was significant because it gave the United States the sole rights to the use of the Pago Pago harbor. The 1889 General Act was an agreement among Great Britain, Germany, the United States, and the Sāmoan Government that assured "security of the life, property and trade of the citizens and subjects of their respective Governments residing in, or having commercial relations with the Islands of Sāmoa" while also binding the parties "at the same time to avoid all occasions of dissensions between their respective Governments and people of Sāmoa, promoting as far as possible the peaceful and orderly civilization of the people of these islands" (Faleomavaega 2014, website).

The Tripartite Convention of 1899 and the Treaty of Berlin renounced British and German rights in the eastern Sāmoa Islands. The repeated refrain of letters written to British and American governments by the various sitting Sāmoan kings, prior to the Berlin Conference, was a plea for protection of lands and people—a protectorate exchange for the exclusive use of the Pago Pago harbor and lands for the Navy's coaling stations directly in line with the trans-Pacific trading routes. After the high chiefs witnessed the collection of heavily armed naval ships at the Apia harbor prepped for battle, they recognized the unrelenting desire of the US military to have Pago Pago harbor (Gilson 1970, p. 221; Ryden 1933, p. 195). On April 17, 1900, the high chiefs ceded the islands of Tutuila and Aunu'u. Four years later, on July 16, 1904, the islands of Tā'u, Olosega, Ofu, and Rose were ceded to the United States (ASCA sec. 2 (1981) [48 USC § 1661]).

In the preamble to the Tutuila and Aunu'u Deeds of Cession, the intention of the high chiefs is clear:

> for the promotion of the peace and welfare of the people of said islands, for the establishment of a good and sound government, and for the preservation of the rights and property of the inhabitants of said islands, the chiefs, rulers and people thereof are desirous of granting unto the said government of the United States full powers and authority to enact proper legislation for and to control the said islands... (ASCA sec. 2 (1981) [48 U.S.C. § 1661])

In the 1904 Deeds of Cession of Manu'a, King Tui Manu'a and the high chiefs of the Manu'a group articulated these same principles. The preamble and section (2) read in part:

> And Whereas, Tuimanu'a and his chiefs, being content and satisfied with the justice, fairness, and wisdom of the government as hitherto administered by the several Commandants of the United States Naval Station, Tutuila, and the officials appointed to act with the Commandant, are desirous of placing the Islands of Manu'a hereinafter described under the full and complete sovereignty of the United States of America to enable said Islands, with Tutuila and Aunuu, to become a part of the territory of said United States;

> (2) It is intended and claimed by these Present that there shall be no discrimination in the suffrages and political privileges between the present residents of said Islands and citizens of the United States dwelling therein, and also that the rights of the chiefs in each village and of all people concerning their property according to their customs shall be recognized. (ASCA sec. 2 (1981) [48 U.S.C. § 1661])

The US federal machine did not wait for the Manu'a Islands to sign over their allegiance to the United States; the Navy displaced Tui Manu'a from his reign over the Manu'a islands and demanded that the high chiefs obey the "New Government" and High Court decisions via intimidation and threats of force.[3]

US Naval (USN) Commandant Uriel Sebree wrote to the US Assistant Secretary of the Navy in the summer of 1902 reporting that Tui Manu'a and his chiefs had disobeyed a 1902 High Court ruling. Commandant Sebree brought Tui Manu'a's chiefs to Tutuila and admonished them all, stating that Tui Manu'a and the Manu'a islands were under the US flag. "I informed him that all orders must be obeyed," Sebree wrote, "that if Tuimanu'a could not enforce orders, I might have to put someone else in the position, and if necessary, I would send an officer and some men on shore to govern them" (Sebree 1902). The USN Commandant held the Manu'a chiefs in Tutuila on charges of conspiracy because one of Tui Manu'a's chiefs, Tulifua, was a Manu'a District Judge believed by the USN Commandant to be conspiring against the United States on behalf of Tui Manu'a. The USN Commandant and US federal machine did not recognize Tui Manu'a as ruler over the Manu'a Islands, which was a completely distinct political-cultural entity from Tutuila. Sebree went as far as to disregard the Tui Manu'a's nobility and power in the islands, simply treating him as a mere district judge in Manu'a who needed to be reminded of his place within the US body-politic. Once Tutuila and Aunu'u islands had been ceded to the United States, Sebree didn't recognize the Manu'a Islands as a politically autonomous jurisdiction and demanded that Tui Manu'a and every *mātai* title holder there obey the laws of the land. Even more egregious, the United States perpetrated an illegal seizure of the Manu'a Islands through the 1900 Tutuila and Aunu'u Deeds of Cession (Sebree 1902). The USN Commandant wrote, "As a matter of personal convenience, and to save a good deal of tedious and worrying annoyance, I should be glad to receive an order cutting loose from the Manu'a Group, but under the treaty this cannot be done. By the introduced a new land taxation and land registration system. This changeover under the US Department of Defense (Navy) was not easy for the indigenous people. Since land surveys had never been done under the centuries of Spanish occupation, registering unsurveyed lands proved to be onerous and costly (Safford 1905). Surveying land, registering land, and levying taxes on land are profitable ways to collect government revenue. Under the US system, a parcel of land is surveyed, survey pegs or markers identify boundaries, and then the land parcel is given a land use classification (agriculture, urban, etc.) by which the size and type of land is quantified for tax allocations to the US government.

The US Navy considered all unregistered and undeveloped land to be Crown lands, owned by the Spanish government. The military in turn determined that all unregistered and undeveloped land was transferred to the US Navy (Department of Defense). Alienation of lands continued under the US administration. Indigenous people struggled to pay the annual land taxes. If they chose not to survey or register the lands, the US government could rightfully recapture each land parcel. The fundamental difference in the political and legal status of American Sāmoa versus the other territories is the protection of its cultural cornerstone: the customary land tenure system. In its 3000-year history, Sāmoans have never been a landless people, nor have their lands been sold to non-Sāmoans (except for less than three percent freehold lands sold prior to the 1900 Deeds of Cession). The signing of the two Deeds of Cession with the United States explicitly protected against the alienation of lands from the Sāmoan people.

The former Spanish colonies—Guam, Puerto Rico, and the Philippines, all indigenous lands—became Crown Lands belonging to the King of Spain (except for lands of the wealthiest and those of the highest class). The Spanish Crown mandated international trade, using these colonies as trading and production outposts to enrich the monarchy. Spanish colonial rule left the indigenous people beholden to the Spanish Crown and nobility for access and use of lands for agriculture and even for the use of key resources, like water. Landless classes existed under the Spanish Crown in Guam, Puerto Rico, and the Philippines. Access to lands under the Spanish empire for subsistence farming became so dismal that this led to many landless peasants living in the mountains to survive (Bryan 2012, p. 9). Some landlessness developed under the United States due to wartime or economic policies that favored US federal government interests. Cathy Bryan of the University of Maine reveals that during the American Great

Depression of the 1930s, the economically crippled Puerto Rico was entirely neglected. US Congress did not intervene to assist the thousands of Puerto Ricans who were landless and homeless in "Hoovervilles" (Bryan 2012). It wasn't until late in the New Deal era that the landless were offered farming lands under the resettlement programs.

When the smoke cleared after World War II, in Guam there were virtually no survey pegs left from the US Navy surveys and most of the land records were destroyed. This gave US Navy Officers virtually unbridled authority to determine what lands were to be public or private and whether compensation to the Chamorros was necessary for the appropriation of land for military installations (Crocombe 1987, pp. 201–202). Crocombe explains that in Guam lands were primarily taken for military fortification: "Occupied by the Japanese in 1941 and reoccupied by the United States forces in July 1944, Guam became a major military base and forty-eight per cent of the island was taken over for military bases" (Crocombe 1987, p. 214). Most recently, the 2011 Government Accountability Office Report on the Defense Infrastructure in Guam advised the US Congress that the Department of Defense has yet to fully assess the impacts of 39,000 military personnel to be transferred from Okinawa to Guam by 2020 ("The Navy Needs" 2011). It remains unknown how much more land in Guam the Department of Defense will need to accommodate these US servicemen/women.

Notes

1. John Williams Jr. is the son John Williams, founder of the London Missionary Society.
2. Guano Islands Act, 11 Stat. 119, enacted August 18, 1856, 48 USC ch. 8 §§ 1411–1419 reads: "Whenever any citizen of the United States discovers a deposit of guano on any island, rock, or key, not within the lawful jurisdiction of any other government, and not occupied by the citizens of any other government, and takes peaceable possession thereof, and occupies the same, such island, rock, or key may, at the discretion of the President, be considered as appertaining to the United States. The discoverer, or his assigns, being citizens of the United States, may be allowed, at the pleasure of Congress, the exclusive right of occupying such island, rocks, or keys, for the purpose of obtaining guano, and of selling and delivering the same to citizens of the United States, to be used therein, and may be allowed to charge and receive for every ton thereof delivered alongside a vessel, in proper tubs, within reach of ship's tackle, a sum not exceeding $8 per ton

for the best quality, or $4 for every ton taken while in its native place of deposit."

3. "New Government" was a term used by the Commandants in the High Court to distinguish the time before the American government was established in 1900 to the time after the American Government was established.
4. Historically, there has been debate between the congressional-executive and sole-executive powers to enter into international treaties with sovereign countries. Some presidents have entered into treaties without the two-thirds consent of Congress when it was declared without his powers as Commander-in-Chief of the Armed Forces or continuation of a prior treaty. President McKinley used such sole-executive powers to execute the Deeds of Cession to enter into American Sāmoa and ordered the US Department of State vis-à-vis US Department of Navy full powers over the islands.
5. National coverage during this period in *North American Review* had graphically called attention to "America's Interest in China" and "America's Opportunity in Asia."
6. However, there was value placed within the context of Sāmoa custom. Land may be used as a tool in facilitating clan alliances during times of need for food and security.

References

ASCA sec.2 1981 [48 U.S.C. § 1661]).

ASCA Puerto Rico Encyclopedia. Continually Updated. http://www.encyclopediapr.org/ing/article.cfm?ref=13071116.

Adams, Henry. 1896–1904. *History of the United States of America*. New York: C. Scribner's Sons.

Amerika Sāmoa Humanities Council. 2009. *A History of American Sāmoa*. Korea.

Balfour, Michael L. 1964. *The Kaiser and His Times*. Ann Arbor: University of Michigan.

Bryan, Henry F. 2012. Order Issued March 8, 1927.

Constitution of Commonwealth of Puerto Rico, art. II, § 14.

Crocombe, Ron. 1987. *Land Tenure in the Pacific*. 3rd ed. Suva: University of South Pacific.

Dulles, Foster R. 1938. *America in the Pacific: A Century of Expansion*. Boston: Houghton Mifflin Co.

Faleomavaega, Eni. 2014. *Historical Documents, Laws, & Deeds Related to American Sāmoa*. Washington, DC: American Sāmoa Congressional Office. http://www.house.gov/faleomavaega/treaties.html. Accessed 1 January 2014.

Fewkes, Jesse. 1907. *The Aborigines of Porto Rico and Neighboring Islands*. Washington, DC: U.S. Government Print Office.

Gilson, Richard P. 1970. *Sāmoa 1830 to 1900: The Politics of a Multi-Cultural Community*. London: Oxford University Press.
Gray, John A. 1960. *Amerika Sāmoa: A History of American Sāmoa and Its United States Naval Administration*. Annapolis: United States Naval Institute.
Guano Islands Act (1856), 11 Stat. 119, 48 U.S.C. ch. 8 §§ 1411–1419.
Hattori, Anne P. 2001. Guardians of Our Soil: Indigenous Responses to Post-World War II Military Land Appropriation on Guam. In *Farms, Films, and Runways: Perspectives on U.S. Military Bases in the Western Pacific*. Chicago: Imprint Publications.
Hay, John. 1899. John Hay to Joseph Choate, April 12.
Kaplan, Amy. 1994. Cultures of United States Imperialism. In *Left Alone with America*, ed. Amy Kaplan and Donald Pease. Duke: University Press Books.
Kaplan, Amy. 2002. *The Anarchy of Empire in the Making of U.S. Culture*. Cambridge: Harvard University Press.
Kyan, Sinichi. 2001. Military Land Usage in Okinawa. In *Farms, Firms, and Runways: Perspectives on U.S. Military Bases in the Western Pacific*, ed. Eve Armentrout. Chicago: Imprint Publications.
LeFeber, Water. 1998. *The New Empire: An Interpretation of American Expansion, 1860–1898*. 4th ed. Ithaca: Cornell University Press.
Leibowitz, Arnold H. 1989. *Defining Status: A Comprehensive Analysis of United States Territorial Relations*. Norwell: Martinus Nijhoff.
Lemkin, Raphaël. 1944. *Axis Rule in Occupied Europe: Laws of Occupation, Analysis of Government, Proposals for Redress*. New York: Carnegie Endowment for International Peace.
Masterman, Sylvia. 1934. *The Origins of International Rivalry in Sāmoa: 1845–1884*. London: George, Allen & Unwin.
McKinley, William. 1938. John Hay to William McKinley, November 9, 1899.
National Archives. 1898. Record Group 59, M-179, roll 1022, Navy Department to S.D., 30/12/1898, and Cridler memo of 18/1/1899.
Rogers, Robert F. 1995. *Destiny's Landfall: A History of Guam*. Honolulu: University of Hawaii.
Román, Ediberto. 2006. *The Other American Colonies: An International and Constitutional Law Examination of the United States' Nineteenth and Twentieth Century Island Conquests*. Durham: Carolina Academic Press.
Ryden, George H. 1933. *The Foreign Policy of the United States in Relation to Sāmoa*. New Haven: Yale University Press.
Safford, William Edward. 1905. *The Useful Plants of the Island of Guam*. Washington, DC: U.S. Government Printing Office.
Sato, Shosuke. 1886. *History of the Land Question in the United States*. Baltimore: John Hopkins University.
Sebree, Uriel. 1902. Uriel Sebree to U.S. Assistant Secretary of the Navy, April 7.

Silva, Noenoe K. 2004. *Aloha Betrayed: Native Hawaiian Resistance to American Colonialism*. Durham: Duke University Press.

Souder, Paul B. 1987. Guam: Land Tenure in a Fortress. In *Land Tenure in the Pacific*, ed. Ron Crocombe. Fiji: University of South Pacific.

Ntumy, Michael A., ed. 1993. *South Pacific Legal Systems*. Honolulu: University of Hawai'i Press.

Sparrow, Bartholomew H. 2006. *The Insular Cases and the Emergency of American Empire*. Lawrence: University Press of Kansas.

Stayman, Allen P. 2009. U.S. Territorial Policy: Trends and Current Challenges. *Pacific Islands Policy* 5: 5.

Sunia, Fofo. 1988. *The Story of the Legislature of American Sāmoa: In Commemoration of the Golden Jubilee, 1948–1998*. Pago Pago: Legislature of American Sāmoa.

Tansill, Charles C. 1940. *The Foreign Policy of Thomas F. Bayard, 1885–1887*. New York: Fordham University Press.

Treaty of Berlin. 1889, arts. I, VIII, sec. 2, 26 Stat. 1497; Treaty Series 313, June 14.

US Census 2010 Population Count. Annually Updated. http://www.census.gov/2010census/data/.

US Congress. 1875. House. Message from the President Transmitting a Report from the Secretary of State and Accompanying Papers; A.B. Steinberger. Washington, DC: U.S. Govt. Print. Off., 1876. 44th Congress, 1st session. House. Executive document no. 161, 6.

US Const. art. II, § 2, cl. 2.

US Government Accountability Office. 1997. Report to the Chairman, Committee on Resources, House of Representatives, US Insular Areas: Application of the US Constitution. GAO/OGC-98-5, 9, November.

US Government Accountability Office. 1982. Report to the Chairman, Committee on Appropriations, House of Representatives: Alternatives to the Northern Mariana Islands Land Lease, August 19.

US Government Accountability Office. 2011. Report. 11-206 to Congressional Committees, The Navy Needs Better Documentation to Support Its Proposed Military Treatment Facilities on Guam, April.

US Navy Department. 1900. Serial Order No. 540. General Records of the U.S. Department of the Navy, February 19.

Va'ai, Asiata S. 1999. *Sāmoa Faamātai and the Rule of Law*. Apia: National University of Sāmoa.

Wolfe, Patrick. 2006. "Settler Colonialism and the Elimination of the Native." *Journal of Genocide Research* 8 (4): 388.

CHAPTER 4

US Naval Administration of American Sāmoa

Naval Administration Authority

In 1900, President McKinley issued Presidential Executive Order No. 125-A, which delegated control of the American Sāmoan Islands to the Secretary of the Navy. Subsequently, the Navy posted to the Tutuila Naval Station a US Navy (USN) Commandant, who exercised full authority and powers as the Commanding Officer over the US Naval fleet moored at the Pago Pago harbor as well as heading the civil administration over American Sāmoa.

Much of scholarship written about the Naval Administration's control over American Sāmoa has focused on the Sāmoan attempts to protect and preserve traditional customs and traditions through the incorporation of courts and judicial decisions and the Western-style rule of law (Gray 1960; Lyons 2005; Darden 1952). Before 1900, there was only village-based self-government and no centralized government. The Navy established a central government in 1900 and a legislature in 1948. There was no territorial Constitution until the US Department of the Interior took over administration. The Navy established the judicial, legislative, and civil administration for the islands. No judicial branch of the government existed during the entire naval period, except for the Department of the Judiciary, which functioned like the Department of Administrative Services and the Department of Public Works (Morrow 1974, pp. 13–18).

L.-N. Memea Kruse, *The Pacific Insular Case of American Sāmoa*,
https://doi.org/10.1007/978-3-319-69971-4_4

The only governing documents that had direct (and supreme) authority over the Navy in its administration of American Sāmoa were the two Deeds of Cession, which expressly stated the United States was required to respect and protect Sāmoan lands and property in exchange for Sāmoan obedience and allegiance to the United States (Faleomavaega 1995, p. 35; Faleomavaega 2014, website).

The Navy's empire building in American Sāmoa established American law and values, which in some cases overruled Sāmoan customs. Ultimately, US authority demonstrated how western law would reign supreme when it became entangled with culture. Without a locally enacted constitution, written or unwritten, law and authority firmly rested with the Naval Administration. For example, Naval regulations permitted "a grant of a trust to a son or daughter legally married to a non-native" or to "a child of an inter-racial marriage" and "life estate to a grandson where the father was not native" (*Aftufil v. Timoteo,* 3 A.S.R. 395 (1959); *Sapela v. Veevalu,* 1 A.S.R. 124 (1905)). This direct exercise of authority by the Naval Administration trumped the land alienation provisions supposedly established to meet the terms of the Deeds of Cession and subverted the intentions of the US Congress to comply and honor those said terms (Leibowitz 1989, pp. 410–443; Barker 2005).

The Navy's power over the administration and adjudication of the introduced western law, like principles of adverse land possession that require corroboration of testimony, perfectly supported the discourse of empire building. The Navy had ultimate sovereignty, not only in the establishment of law and the way it interacted with culture but also in the adjudication of those laws. The introduction and incorporation of adverse land possession principles are the building blocks of nationalistic empire building, cloaked as an instrument to civilize and standardize Sāmoan society. There was an imbalance between the "individual" versus Sāmoan communal concept by the Navy's emphasis of the individual's right to title. This preference corrodes communal lands available for Sāmoan community land tenure and threatened the *fa'amātai* (So'o 2007; Va'ai 1999). Without traditional lands, *mātai* titles are meaningless.

Law of Convenience and Individual Land Ownership

The Naval Administration introduced western legal concepts that purported to establish "legitimate" jurisprudence under the newly adopted American government. The High Court consisted exclusively of Naval possession (Tiffany 1981, pp. 136–153). The High Court also used this to allow individual claims to prevail over communal claims, leading to the establishment of the idea of individually held lands. Tiffany writes:

> In systems where the traditional rights and obligations of kin have begun to change in response to new economic and political institutions, a legal idea like adverse possession that individualizes land rights and confers security of tenure against other descent group members may enjoy success to the extent that it reflects emerging social norms. Whether the people of American Sāmoa wish to see their traditional land tenure patterns so affected, only they can say. (Tiffany 1981, pp. 136–153)

By examining the gradual progression of these forms of individualist rights splitting communal land holdings and impacting the traditional authority of law, the growing acceptance of the "individual" manifests itself later as incorporation of individually owned lands.

The impact of these changes also involves the acceptance of individually owned lands within the context of Sāmoan lifestyle, together with the political framework that engendered American nationalism within the fabric of indigenous Sāmoan society. Nationalism gave birth to modern imperialism, and the political control of undeveloped regions engineered by colonial superpowers allowed Americans to pursue their colonial role as champions of dollar diplomacy (Ellison 1938, p. 7; Bender 2006, pp. 193–206). Law acted as a state monopoly by which the acceptance of ideology was translated into rules, codes, policies, and statutes (Tamanaha 2001). The amalgamation of law by the Naval Commandants, the federally appointed military-state apparatus, was an essential aspect of the American state-building process. The military's administrative apparatus came to oversee law enforcement, judicial, and executive authority. The constructs of this state legal system assumed monopoly over civil and customary law and legal authority over native lands. Historian and legal historiographer, Donald Kelley, writes that "customary law" progresses in accordance with the mechanisms, modes, requirements, and interests of legal administrators and the legal system (Kelley 1990, p. 106). In other words, "customary law" as understood by legal authorities does not necessarily correlate to actual customs. Adverse possession rights have led to the exponential growth of individual land ownership that is antithetical to *fa'amātai* culture and *fa'asāmoa* value system.

The application and usage of adverse possession in American Sāmoa allows an individual person to stake a claim to real property based upon various elements of possession. Actual possession required that all claimants provide evidence through testimony and corroboration, hostile possession required physical occupancy over a requisite period, open and exclusive possession required conspicuous occupation that leaves no doubt regarding ownership by village residents, and notorious possession required the opportunity for the true owner to learn that his supposed land has an adverse claim upon it (Kelley 1990, p. 26). The Navy's intention in introducing adverse possession in American Sāmoa statute was to legitimize the ownership of privately owned land. Sāmoa's late Minister of Parliament, Asiata A.V. Sale'imoa Va'ai, describes how Sāmoan land tenure uses principles of lineage, access, and use rather than ownership:

> The principle difference between custom and the market is that, in the former, land is regarded as an object firmly embedded in social (and metaphysical) relationships, while the latter views land as a commodity and a factor of production ... Authority or *pule* is the central principle that governs Sāmoan land ownership and other customary property. (Va'ai 1999, p. 47)

Va'ai describes the nature of individualized ownership of native land and the customary traditions still within the Sāmoan context of traditional customary land tenure:

> ... the new individualized ownership of land is the traditional concept of *pulefaaaoga* or exploitative authority which gives the occupants—individuals—the rights to control and use family land being occupied and allotted for their use. Land allocated, may moreover continue to remain in the exclusive possession and use of several generations of a particular member or members but ownership remains in the extended family and under its constitutive authority. This is due to the established principle of Sāmoan customary land that all family land is owned by the corporate structure in perpetuity. 'What property exists is vested in the family, not in the individual.' As Chief Justice Tiavaasue also stated: Customary land does not land belonging to individuals. Land is under the Protective authority of the Alii and Faipule. Subject to this is the Pule of the *mātai* which authorizes the exploitation and usage of family land. The individual has no land, it is land given by the village to the *mātai*. Just because the individual occupies and uses the land it is not his to own (translation). (Va'ai 1999, p. 49)

An individual does not own communal land but rather by the village and/or *āiga*, and no title is given, because the land is not owned by any one person or *mātai*. In Roman society, *dominium* or *jus utendi* was understood as the right to use and enjoy or abuse and destroy—this term has been used to embolden the ownership of things with the view of *dominium* in Roman law (Paterson and Farran 2004, p. 26). The Western concept of land ownership is contradictory to the Sāmoan concept of land ownership. Dominium or ownership as an absolute power over land, things, or even possibly a person, allowed the owner to do as he desired with land—or with a person (Paterson and Farran 2004, p. 26).

Professor of law Susan Farran writes that land ownership in the twentieth century is best defined as "ownership as the ultimate right to the enjoyment of a thing, as fully as the State permits, when all prior rights in that thing vested in persons other than the one entitled to ultimate use, by way of encumbrance, have been exhausted" (Paterson and Farran 2004, p. 27). For land ownership, this type of land possession goes directly against the Sāmoan customary sense of land use and occupation. The late New Zealand diplomat and last Governor of Sāmoa Sir Guy Powles describes the tenure of customary land in Sāmoa:

> In customary law terms, an interest in customary land is held by an individual through the *aiga* of which he is a member. Membership of the group, which might include several nuclear families, is determined by heredity, relationship by marriage, and personal service to the group and to the *mātai*. Thus, land is vested beneficially in that group of family members who are for the time being living and working on it, or contributing to it, and who are serving the *pule*, or authority, of the chiefly title to which the land pertains. Land is regarded as appurtenant to the title of the *mātai* of the family, who is responsible for administering the title on behalf of the family. (Powles 1993, p. 419)

Within the South Pacific region, adverse land possession by way of occupation over a period of time has ultimately conferred ownership to the possessor, thus giving case law authority to the concept of privately owned land (*Tada v. Usa* [1996] SBHC 7, *SMEC v. Temeakamwaka Landowners* [1998] KICA 4, *Kippion v. Attorney General* [1994] VUSC 1). The notion of acquiring title by adverse possession of land in English common law is based on exclusivity of possession, which entitles the holder of the possessory right to use it and protect it against all other claimants. USN Naval Commandant Charles Moore, who was appointed Governor of American Sāmoa in 1905, stated, "It is not worthwhile for this Court to cite the numberless authorities on the question of the settlement of titles by adverse possession. ***The doctrine is so well understood that it is a waste of time to discuss it***" (emphasis added) (*Talala v. Logo*, 1 A.S.R. 166, 171 (1907)). This kind of speech and attitude encapsulates the Naval Court's rationale for incorporating western legal concepts without deliberate consideration of the consequences to the Sāmoan political, social, or cultural structure. The *papālagis* erroneously considered these concepts to be vital to the welfare of "American" Sāmoan society through the legal systems of western jurisprudence. Nation-building was advanced through the apparatus of the legal institution which in American Sāmoa was also the administrative-civil arm of governance. There were no branches of government.

US expansion into the Pacific was also a means of economic growth for nation-building empire projects, and an explicit benefit of adverse ownership was the development of land productivity and the acquisition of lands for commerce. Historian David Hanlon proclaims that in American Sāmoa where there was conflict between American administrative law and policy and *fa'asāmoa* values and traditions, American law reigned supreme (Hanlon 1994, pp. 93–118).

The "Law of Convenience" provided a legally acceptable foundation to assert the supremacy of individually owned land rights. The principles of adverse land possession have been incorporated into American Sāmoa as acceptable practice to claim land, regardless of whether that land is communally occupied or virgin bush land. The acceptance of these land principles in law and in society have allowed the general acceptance of the conversion of communal lands into individually owned lands and privately owned that is unconnected to *fa'asāmoa* (Leibowitz 1989, p. 431). Adverse possession rights are an ultimate threat to the terms of the Deeds of Cession, which specifically require that Sāmoan lands and the entire structure of Sāmoan culture be respected and protected. The Deeds of Cession are comparable in some respects to the 1840 Treaty of Waitangi, through which the Māori chiefs of Aotearoa (New Zealand) ceded formal sovereignty of their islands to Great Britain but also protected their rights to their indigenous lands and to self-governance (Cleave 1989, pp. 74–78).[2] The Waitangi Treaty is now constitutionally vital, as the rights of the Māoris as spelled out within the treaty must be considered by the New Zealand government prior to any major decision concerning Māori land.

Land Tenure

Extended families reside under the leadership of designated member(s) whom they select to hold the family's *mātai* (chief) title. In American Sāmoa, *tautua* (service) and *pule* (authority) over communal land always rests with senior *mātai* of the family (*Taufa'asau v. Mauga* A.S.R. (1979)). The *mātai* title comes from a consensus of the *āiga*, which has stewardship over communal lands. From the early missionary days, the communal nature of traditional Sāmoan land ownership was thought to be a hindrance to progress; historian George Turner exclaimed that the Sāmoan "communistic system is a sad hindrance to the industrious and eats like a canker worm at the roots of individual and national progress" (Turner 1884, p. 161). The *papālagis'* incomplete understanding of the stratified communal system may have also led them to perceive Sāmoans as not industrious. Edward Bicknell describes Sāmoans as, "The people are of the pure Polynesian race, and are very much like lazy, good-natured children. Gay, kind, pleasure-loving, and fairly intelligent, they are easily excited, but not revengeful" (Bicknell 1904, p. 119).

Land Categorization

Land is considered the most important tangible asset of the Sāmoan people and has traditionally been the central basis for family organization and family identity and a mechanism for sustaining villages in a subsistence society. Land is passed from one generation to the next within the *āiga*; the *mātai* title holder has control over the land and assigns holdings to family members.

Five categories comprise the traditional land tenure system today. First, "freehold lands" are all lands acquired by court grants prior to the 1900s which at the request of the owner have not been returned to the status of other land tenure classifications.[3] The American Sāmoa 2013 Statistical Yearbook lists 1072 registered freehold acres (American Sāmoa Statistical Yearbook 2013, p. 98). Private ownership of freehold land is comparable to the fee title system (but not identical), and there are no restrictions on transfer of title or lease tenure. Freehold lands in American Sāmoa are mostly located in Pago Pago, Tafuna, and Leone.

Second, "government-owned lands" are lands that may be conveyed freely to the American Sāmoa Government from the federal government or from native owners for governmental purposes (*Mulu v. Taliutafa*, 3

A.S.R. 82 (1953)).[4] There are 1651 registered government-owned acres in 2013 (American Samoa Statistical Yearbook 2013, p. 175). Government lands may be acquired by eminent domain through condemnation proceedings, right of way easements, and reclamations.

Third, "church-owned lands" can be acquired through court grants and conveyance by native owners with the consent of the Governor. Church-owned lands total 1030 registered acres (American Samoa Statistical Yearbook 2013, p. 175). The leasing of church lands to parties other than the American Sāmoa Government requires the approval of the Governor. Transfer of church lands to non-American Sāmoans is prohibited by law, and the reconveyance and retransfer of church lands shall be to native American Sāmoans only, again at the discretion of and with approval by the Governor.

Fourth, "individually owned lands" has been construed by judicial rulings as land that shows evidence of cultivation and continuous occupancy that can be owned by an individual, completely distinct from a village or *mātai*.[5] Individually owned land is a hybrid land classification that is not fee simple and not freehold. There are 2029 registered individually owned acres, which include land acquired by an individual through court action after the year 1900, through the transfer of communal land to an individual with the approval of the Governor or through the window of opportunity supported by adverse land possession (American Samoa Statistical Yearbook 2013, pp. 97–108).

Lastly, "communal or native lands" are held by extended Sāmoan families and are subject to the authority of the *mātai*. There are 2106 registered communal acres (American Samoa Statistical Yearbook 2013, pp. 97–108). This authority does not imply fee ownership. Rather, it is a form of stewardship over native lands that allow *mātai* to allocate land to the *āiga* network.

The 8367 unregistered acres are, in theory, open to being converted into individually owned lands under the current land use tenure system. According to the 2013 Statistical Yearbook, there is only a one percent difference between communally owned and individually owned lands, and soon, registered individually owned acreage will outnumber lands registered for communal use. Since 2003, the total area of registered communally owned acreage has grown by 72 acres for all 11 districts in American Sāmoa, while the registered individually owned lands have grown by 126 acres. More people are registering individually owned lands for themselves than there are registered communally owned lands for the village and *āiga* use.

An "I" attitude, otherwise known as "individual" identity and rights as a "person," is at odds with the communal lifestyle and traditional system of land tenure in American Sāmoa (Coulter 1957, p. 83). The stewardship over land within the context of Sāmoan culture is not permanent; it exists only if the current *mātai* permits it. Communal lands provide the means for Sāmoan traditions to survive by providing villages spaces for customary structures reserved for *mātai (faletalimālō)*, *malae* (open land reserved for greeting visitors, playing sports, and village gatherings), and homes built on land allocated to each family. Additionally, communal lands provide access to forestry and soil for building homes and traditional meeting houses, access to agriculture, access to streams and fruit trees for domestic consumption and cultural exchanges, and access to lands for farming activity. Furthermore, communal lands carry no property taxes. As more and more lands are converted from communal (native) lands into individually owned lands, less and less space is available in the near and distant future for extended families to use to farm lands or spaces to host extended family members, access to food for family and village purposes, and for people residing in each village to provide service toward the *fa'amātai*. Individually owned land curtails the availability of communal lands for future generations and will ultimately result in the death of Sāmoan culture.

Notes

1. Brian A. Garner, *Black's Law Dictionary* (St. Paul: West Group, 1996), 22; Sue Farran and Don Paterson, *South Pacific Property Law* (London: Cavendish Publishing, 2004), 166–167; ASCA § 37.0120 (1982); *Magalei v. Atualevao*, 19 ASR 2d 86 (1991); *Willis v. Faiivae*, 17 ASR 2d 38 (1990); *Salavea v. Ilaoa*, 2 ASR 15 (1986); *Tuiolosega, v. Voa*, 2 ASR 138 (1941); *Sei v. Aumavae*, 2 ASR 396 (1948); *Soliai v. Lagafua*, 2 ASR 436 (1949); *Sione v. Tiualii*, 3 ASR 66 (1963); *Ofoia v. Pritchard*, 4 ASR 326 (1963); *Fau v. Wilson*, 4 A.S.R. 443 (1964); *Lolo v. Heirs of Sekio*, 4 ASR 477 (1964); *Lualemana v. Atualevao*, 16 ASR 2d 34 (1990).
2. Waitangi Treaty is named after the Treaty House on Waitangi Bay, Bay of Islands in (Northern) New Zealand, where the Treaty was signed affording Māoris with protections to their indigenous lands. What is also noteworthy about this Treaty is the symbolism attached to the intent or meaning of this document. Waitangi means 'weeping waters' in the Māori language.

3. In *Willis v. Faiivae*, 17 SASR 2d 38 (1990), it reads, "The court is bound by statute and treaty to recognize freehold grants made by the Land Commission of Sāmoa, which operated in Apia under the supervision of the then-Supreme Court of Sāmoa, prior to the United States-established government." ASCA. § 37.0201(b) (1999) and *Vaiao v. Craddick*, 14 ASR 2d 108 (1990), freehold land is all those lands included in court grants prior to 1900.
4. *Mulu v. Taliutafa,* 3 ASR 82 (1953), at the time of cession of Sāmoa to United States, public property passed to United States Government and not Government of Sāmoa.
5. *Taatiatia v. Misi*, 2 ASR 46 (1948); *Muli v. Ofoia*, 2 ASR 408, 410 (1948); *Soliai v. Lagafua*, 2 ASR 436 (1949); *Fa'atiliga v. Fano,* 2 ASR 376 (1948); *Gi v. Te'o*, 3 ASR 570 (1961); *Magalei v. Lualemaga* 4 ASR 242 (1962); *Government v. Letuli*, No. 016-63 (1963); *Haleck v. Tuia*, LT No. 1386-74 (1974); *Fanene v. Talio*, LT No. 64–77 (1977).

References

American Sāmoa Government v. Haleck, LT 10-08, slip op. (Trial Div. May 1, 2013).

Aftufil v. Timoteo, 3 A.S.R. 395 (1959).

Kaliopa v. Silao, 2 A.S.R. 2d 1 (1983).

Kippion v. Attorney General [1994] VUSC 1.

Mulu v. Taliutafa, 3 A.S.R. 82 (1953).

SMEC v. Temeakamwaka Landowners [1998] KICA 4.

Sapela v. Veevalu, 1 A.S.R. 124 (1905).

Tada v. Usa, [1996] SBHC 7.

Talala v. Logo, 1 A.S.R. 165 (1907).

Taufaasau v. Mauga, A.S.R. (1979).

A.S.C.A. 37.0204, readopted 1980; PL 16-88 §§ 1, 2.

Public Law 7-19 § 9.0103 (1962).

So'o, Asofou, ed. 2007. *Changes in the Mātai System: O Suiga I le Fa'amātai.* Apia: Centre for Sāmoan Studies.

Barker, Joanne, ed. 2005. *Sovereignty Matters: Locations of Contestation and Possibility in Indigenous Struggles for Self-Determination.* Lincoln: University of Nebraska.

American Sāmoa Government Department of Commerce. *Statistical Yearbook* 2013. Published Annually. http://www.doc.as.gov. Accessed 5 January 2013.

Bender, Thomas. 2006. *A Nation Among Nations: America's Place in World History.* New York: Hill and Wang.

Bicknell, Edward. 1904. *The Territorial Acquisitions of the United States 1787–1904.* Boston: Small, Maynard & Company.

Cleave, Peter. 1989. *The Sovereignty Game: Power, Knowledge, and Reading the Treaty*. Wellington: Victoria University Press.

Coulter, John W. 1957. *The Pacific Dependencies of the United States*. New York: Macmillan Company.

Darden, Joe T. 1952. *Historical Sketch of the Naval Administration of the Government of American Sāmoa, April 17, 1900–July 1, 1951*. Washington, DC: Department of Navy.

Ellison, Joseph. 1938. *Opening and Penetration of Foreign Influence in Sāmoa to 1880*. Corvalis: Oregon State College.

Faleomavaega, Eni. 1995. *Navigating the Future: A Samoan Perspective on U.S.-Pacific Relations*. Suva: University of South Pacific.

Faleomavaega, Eni. 2014. *Historical Documents, Laws, & Deeds Related to American Sāmoa*. Washington, DC: American Sāmoa Congressional Office. http://www.house.gov/faleomavaega/treaties.html.

Gray, John A. 1960. *Amerika Sāmoa: A History of American Sāmoa and Its United States Naval Administration*. Annapolis: United States Naval Institute.

Hanlon, David. 1994. Patterns of Colonial Rule in Micronesia. In *Tides of History: The Pacific Islands in the Twentieth Century*, ed. Kerry R. Howe, Robert C. Kiste, and Brij V. Lal. Honolulu: University of Hawai'i Press.

Kelley, Donald. 1990. *The Human Measure: Social Thought in the Western Legal Tradition*. Cambridge: Harvard University Press.

Leibowitz, Arnold H. 1989. *Defining Status: A Comprehensive Analysis of United States Territorial Relations*. Norwell: Martinus Nijhoff.

Lyons, Paul. 2005. *American Pacificism: Oceania in the U.S. Imagination*. New York: Routledge.

Morrow, Arthur. 1974. *My Thirty-Two Years in American Samoa*.

Paterson, Don, and Sue Farran. 2004. *South Pacific Property Law*. London: Cavendish Publishing.

Powles, Guy. 1993. *South Pacific Island Legal Systems*. Honolulu: University of Hawai'i Press.

Tamanaha, Brian Z. 2001. *A General Jurisprudence of Law and Society*. Oxford: Oxford University Press.

Tiffany, Walter W. 1981. "The Applicability of Western Judicial Concepts to Polynesian Land Disputes: High Court Use of the Adverse Possession Principle in American Sāmoa." *Oceania* 52 (2): 136–153.

Turner, George. 1884. *Sāmoa: A Hundred Years Ago and Long Before*. London: Macmillan and Co.

Va'ai, Asiata S. 1999. *Sāmoa Faamātai and the Rule of Law*. Apia: National University of Sāmoa.

CHAPTER 5

Ex Proprio Vigore and the Insular Cases

Between 1898 and 1905, American imperialists were pitted against anti-imperialists in the "great debate" over expansion beyond the US continent (Welch 1972). The US expansionist period began with the Spanish War of 1898. The Treaty of Paris in 1898 between the United States and Spain ceded Guam and Puerto Rico to the United States. The United States purchased the Philippines for $20 million, while Cuba was acquired under protectorate status (Coletta 1961, pp. 341–350). Also in this decade, Hawai'i was annexed and the United States was pushing for a canal site in Central America. Senator Orville Platt's position was that America had the burden to provide these (formerly Spanish) far-flung territories access to liberty that only America could provide. President William McKinley's proclamation of "benevolent assimilation" came during the US Senate's debate on the ratification of the Treaty of Paris (Miller 1982; Bender 2006, pp. 182–187).

National debate seethed over where America's "sphere of influence" should expand outside of its borders, turning the 1900 Presidential election into a referendum on colonialism. The expansionists cited Rudyard Kipling's "White Man's Burden" as further evidence of the duty and moral obligation of *papālagi* to civilize and govern these alien and backward races including Filipinos, Cubans, Puerto Ricans, and Hawai'ians. Debates emerged over the constitutional status of insular (island) territories and what was or was not "a desirable possession." In 1897, the Supreme Court's observation that ter-

L.-N. Memea Kruse, *The Pacific Insular Case of American Sāmoa*,
https://doi.org/10.1007/978-3-319-69971-4_5

ritories were "inhabited by alien races, differing from us in religion, customs, laws, methods of taxation and modes of thought"[1] compelled the reconsideration of the political and administrative status of insular territories.

Ex Proprio Vigore and the Insular Cases

Three opinions concerning the legal morass of the US Congress to acquire and govern territories emerged as early as 1898 (even before the Treaty of Paris debates) in the *Harvard Law Review*. These opinions created the legal groundwork for the flag-Constitution issue, which would be used later by the US Supreme Court in deciding the insular cases. Elmer Adams and Carman F. Randolph proposed that the Constitution follows the flag "ex proprio vigore," whatever territory was absorbed into the US body-politic, the Constitution and all its rights and privileges automatically followed (Randolph and Adams 1898, pp. 292–315). The supporters of ex proprio vigore contended that statehood and extension of rights must be a condition of territorial acquisition. Contrarily, Christopher C. Langdell and others in the government argued, as War Secretary Elihu Root did, that the Constitution follows the flag but does not "quite catch up" (Langdell 1899, pp. 365–392). Langdell and pro-imperialists claimed that Congress had plenary powers to act in whatever way it should choose. The compromise came from Harvard's professor of government Abbott L. Lowell. Lowell argued that Congress could not do whatsoever it chose but was also not limited to automatically or austerely applying the Constitution. The US Congress, through its treaty-making powers, could choose to take one of two paths. It could incorporate the territory, as it had done with the Northwest Territory and Hawai'i. Or it could keep the territory as unincorporated, which the Congress planned to do with Puerto Rico, the Philippines, and Guam.

Introducing the slippery semantic slope—the two-class "incorporated and unincorporated status" bequeathed to insular territories—provided the US Congress a legal loophole.

It was in this sociopolitical atmosphere that the insular cases were born. The US Supreme Court (and a District Court one-off case) decided these cases, which determined two schemes of insular territorial acquisition: (1) for incorporated territories, the Constitution applies ex proprio vigore or of its own force and (2) for unincorporated territories strictly "fundamental" constitutional rights and privileges apply. Table 5.1 demonstrates how imprecise the formula for determining "incorporated" and "unincorporated" was as it was laid out in the following insular cases:

Table 5.1 Insular cases overview

US Supreme Court—insular case	*Congressional act*	*Insular case—argument*	*US Supreme Court/ Appellate Court/or District Court decision*	*US Supreme Court "doctrines" majority*	*US Supreme Court "doctrines" dissenting*
Downes v. Bidwell (182 US 244, 45 L. Ed. 1088, 21 S. Ct. 770 (1901)	Foraker Act (1900)—established civil government for Puerto Rico. Also explicitly authorized the imposition of duties on goods entering or leaving Puerto Rico, including merchandise moving immediately to or from any US state. (Act of Apr. 12, 1900, ch. 191, 31 Stat. 77.)	Plaintiff argued that the duty and the portion of the Foraker Act authorizing it violated the uniformity clause, which requires that "all Duties, Imposts, and Excises shall be uniform throughout all the United States. (US Const., art I. 8, para.1) Also argued that the Act contravened the revenue clause, "[N]or shall Vessels bound to, or from, one State, be obliged to enter, clear, or pay Duties in another." (US Const., art I. § 9, para. 6)	Upheld the duty and the Act. Holding that US Congress is not required to treat Puerto Rico uniformly for the purpose of duties, imports, and excises (as it does the continental states).	**Justice White's winning "Incorporation Doctrine"**—Both White's and Brown's doctrines concluded that while not all provisions of constitution applied, some basic principles would apply ex proprio vigore. However, White situated the issue as hinging on whether or not Puerto Rico, at the time of the passage of the tax levy, had "been incorporated into and forms a part of the United States." (182 US 292.)	**Justice Brown's 'Extension Doctrine'**—He believed that the revenue clauses were not applicable in Puerto Rico, nor binding upon Congress in legislating with respect to the island. "Congress manifestly must intend that the Constitution apply to a territory before every provision of the document is effective there." (182 US at 270–271, 283–286.)
Hawaii v. Mankichi, 190 US 197, 47 L. Ed. 1016, 23 S. Ct. 787 (1903)	N/A	Application of the Fifth Amendment guarantee of a grand jury indictment and Sixth Amendment guarantee of a jury trial in territories. Mankichi had been convicted of manslaughter in Hawai'i. Statutory law after annexation provided conviction without indictment and by a less than unanimous 12-member jury.	Conviction of Mankichi upheld.	**Justice Brown "Opinion of the Court"**—Constitution had not been extended to Hawai'i based upon the Congressional resolution annexing Hawai'i to the United States (217–218) [Extension Doctrine revisited]; holding that the Fifth and Sixth Amendment rights were not fundamental.	**Justice White**—Hawai'i was not incorporated (only annexed) by the United States; holding that the Fifth and Sixth Amendment rights were not fundamental.

(*continued*)

Table 5.1 (continued)

US Supreme Court—insular case	*Congressional act*	*Insular case—argument*	*US Supreme Court/ Appellate Court/or District Court decision*	*US Supreme Court "doctrines" majority*	*US Supreme Court "doctrines" dissenting*
DeLima v. Bidwell, 182 US 1, 45 L. Ed. 1041, 2 St. Ct. 743 (1901)	N/A	Application that the Port of New York City had no jurisdiction to collect duties on sugar imported from Puerto Rico (after 1899) because Puerto Rico was annexed to the United States.	Upon ratification of the Treaty of Paris, Puerto Rico was not a foreign country for purposes of the tariff laws of the United States, which required payment of duties on goods moving into the United States from a foreign country.	**Justice Brown "Opinion of the Court**—We are therefore of opinion that at the time these duties were levied Porto Rico was not a foreign country within the meaning of the tariff laws, but a territory of the United States, that the duties were illegally exacted and that the plaintiffs are entitled to recover them back.	**Justice White**—Settle whether Porto Rico is "foreign country" or "domestic territory," to use the antithesis of the opinion of the court, and, it is said you settle the controversy in this litigation. But in what sense, foreign or domestic? Abstractly and unqualifiedly, to the full extent that those words imply, or limitedly, in the sense that the word "foreign" is used in the customs laws of the United States? If abstractly, the case turns upon a definition, and the issue becomes single and simple, presenting no difficulty, and yet the arguments at bar have ranged over all the powers of government, and this court divides in opinion. If at the time the duties which are complained of were levied, Porto Rico was as much a foreign country as it was before the war with Spain; if it was as much domestic territory as New York now is, there would be no serious controversy in the case. If the former, the terms and the intention of the Dingley act would apply. If the latter, whatever its words or intention, it could not be applied. Between these extremes there are other relations, and that Porto Rico occupied one of them, and its products hence were subject to duties under the Dingley Tariff act, can be demonstrated. Indeed, we have the authority of a member of the majority of the court, and the organ of the court's opinion in this case, that even if Porto Rico were domestic territory its products could be legally subjected to tariff duties.

Table 5.1 (continued)

US Supreme Court—insular case	*Congressional act*	*Insular case—argument*	*US Supreme Court/ Appellate Court/or District Court decision*	*US Supreme Court "doctrines" majority*	*US Supreme Court "doctrines" dissenting*
Balzac v. Porto Rico, 258 US 298, 66 L. Ed. 627, 42 S. Ct. 343 (1922)	Jones Act (1917): an organic law for Puerto Rico granting full US citizenship to all Puerto Ricans who desired it. Also created a statutory Bill of Rights including guarantees of the first eight amendments.	Application of Sixth Amendment right to jury trial in Porto Rico. Porto Rico criminal procedure disallowed a grand jury in misdemeanor cases.	Sixth Amendment protections do not apply to unincorporated territories of the United States.	**Unanimous decision**—CJ Taft stated that although the Jones Act had granted citizenship to Puerto Ricans, it had not incorporated Puerto Rico. Although Puerto Rico had been under the control of the United States since 1898, the territory had not been designated for ultimate statehood, and Congress could determine which parts of the Constitution would apply. Taft distinguished Puerto Rico from the territory in the Alaska purchase, acquired from Russia in 1867, which had been held to be incorporated in Rasmussen v. United States. (306–307)	N/A
Rassmussen v. United States, 192 US 516, 49 L. Ed. 862, 25 S. Ct. 1893, (1905)	N/A	Application of Sixth Amendment rights was circumvented because of Alaska's criminal procedure.	Reversed misdemeanor conviction for maintaining a place of prostitution.	**Justice White "Opinion of the Court" (no dissent, concurring opinions)**—Found that Alaska had been "incorporated" into the Union, and, based on the Incorporation Doctrine, looked at the intent of Congress granting the territorial inhabitants "all the rights, advantages and immunities of citizens of the United States" found in the treaty between the United States and Russia over the acquisition of Alaska. (197 US at 522) Holding void provision of Act of June 6, 1900 § 171.	N/A

(*continued*)

Table 5.1 (continued)

US Supreme Court—insular case	*Congressional act*	*Insular case—argument*	*US Supreme Court/ Appellate Court/or District Court decision*	*US Supreme Court "doctrines" majority*	*US Supreme Court "doctrines" dissenting*
Reid v. Covert, 354 US 1, 1 L. Ed. 2d 1148, 77 S. Ct. 1222 (1957)	N/A	Application of Sixth Amendment rights to a trial by jury.	The Constitution supersedes all treaties ratified by the US Senate. The military may not try the civilian wife of a soldier under military jurisdiction.	**Justice Harlan "Concurring Opinion of the Court to reverse on rehearing"**—Justice Harlan's concurrence was premised on the idea that the Constitution applies overseas, unless its application was "impracticable and anomalous." He found that providing Fifth Amendment rights extraterritorially was impracticable and anomalous. Justice Harlan and Frankfurter agreed territorial cases to mean "not that the Constitution 'does not apply' overseas, but that there are provisions in the Constitution which do not *necessarily* apply in all circumstances in every foreign place." *Id* at 74. In the Insular Cases, "there is no rigid … rule that Congress, as a condition precedent to exercising power over Americans overseas, must exercise it subject to all the guarantees of the Constitution, no matter what the conditions and considerations are that would make adherence to a specific guarantee altogether ***impractical*** and ***anomalous***." 354 US at 74 (emphasis added)	**Justices Clark and Burton "Dissent"—No reversal on rehearing.** Declared that civilian dependents of US servicemen may constitutionally be tried by an American military court-martial in a foreign country for an offense committed in that country. Stating "Congress has provided in Article 2(11) of the Uniform Code of Military Justice, 64 Stat. 109, 50 USC 552 (1), that they shall be so tried in those countries with which we have an implementing treaty." The question therefore is whether this enactment is reasonably related to the power of Congress "to make Rules for the Government and Regulation of the land and Naval forces." US Const., Art. I § 8, cl. 14.

(*continued*)

Table 5.1 (continued)

US Supreme Court—insular case	*Congressional act*	*Insular case—argument*	*US Supreme Court/ Appellate Court/or District Court decision*	*US Supreme Court "doctrines" majority*	*US Supreme Court "doctrines" dissenting*
King v. Morton, 172 US App. D.C. 126, 520 F. 2d 1140 (1975)	No Congressional Act. *Balzac v. Porto Rico* set the precedent that jury trials in unincorporated territories were not required under the US Constitution.	Application of Sixth Amendment rights to a trial by jury.	The court of appeals remandedthe case back to the district court to determine if a jury trial in American Sāmoa would be impractical oranomalous. 520 F. 2d at 1147.	**Appellate court** emphasized, "a decision in this case [must] rest on a solid understanding of the present legal and cultural development of American Sāmoa. That understanding cannot be based on unsubstantiated opinion; it must be based on facts." **"Specifically, it must be determined whether the Sāmoan mores and *mātai* culture with its strict societal distinctions will accommodate a jury system in which a defendant is tried before his peers; whether a jury in Sāmoa could fairly determine the facts of a case in accordance with the instructions of the court without being unduly influenced by customs and traditions of which the criminal law takes no notice; and whether the implementation of a jury system would be practicable. In short, the question is whether in American Sāmoa circumstances are such that trial by jury would be impractical and anomalous.**" (emphasis added) 520 F.2d at 1147	**Appellate court dissent,** balancing the stronger presumption that favored the application of constitutional provisions in a territory, like American Sāmoa. 520 F.2d at 1156–1161.

(*continued*)

Table 5.1 (continued)

US Supreme Court—insular case	*Congressional act*	*Insular case—argument*	*US Supreme Court/ Appellate Court/or District Court decision*	*US Supreme Court "doctrines" majority*	*US Supreme Court "doctrines" dissenting*
Remand of King v. Morton to King v. Andrus, 452 F. Supp. 11 (D.D.C. 1977).	No Congressional Act. *Balzac v. Porto Rico* laid the grounds whereas jury trials in unincorporated territories were not required under the US Constitution.	Application of Sixth Amendment rights to a trial by jury.	Revised Code of American Sāmoa, Rules of the High Court of American Sāmoa and the rules and regulations of the Secretary of Interior, which deny the right of trial by jury in criminal cases in American Sāmoa are unconstitutional, and the defendant is permanently enjoined from enforcing any judgment of criminal conviction against plaintiff obtained without according him a right to trial by jury. The District Court for the District of Columbia determined that jury trials in criminal cases would not be impractical or anomalous in the territory and imposed the use of such trials in the territory.	Majority opinion—"The fact is that all of the hard evidence which bears on the actual situation in American Sāmoa today in terms of its legal and cultural development cuts the other way, and leads me to the inescapable conclusion that trial by jury in American Sāmoa as of the time when Jake King went to trial on the criminal charges here involved would not have been, and is not now, 'impractical and anomalous'." *Id* at 20	

Downes is the landmark case because it was the first time that the US Supreme Court directly addressed whether provisions of the Constitution affect Congressional legislation in the insular areas. Under *Downes*, the conflict was over the 1900 Foraker Act, which authorized a duty that violated the Constitutional Uniformity Clause (U.S. Const. art. I § 8). The justices agreed that the Constitution is operative in connection to the express powers of the US Congress over the insular areas, but, as Justice White declared, the more relevant question was whether Puerto Rico was incorporated "into and forms a part of the United States" (182 U.S. at 292). Examining the concurring opinion, the justices probed the treaty with France that settled the Louisiana Purchase. The majority opinion specifies that incorporation must be preceded by the intent of Congress to endow statehood. Dissenting Chief Justice Fuller discounts this kind of legalese because citizenship was not on the table for the insular areas in question, particularly in Puerto Rico, and therefore incorporation requiring the precipitation of statehood by the US Congress was in effect a dead end for these insular areas (Cabranes 1978, pp. 427–428). Fuller realized that applying the language of "Congressional intentions" to the incorporation of these foreign lands meant that they might never become incorporated unless the US Congress expressed its intent to do so. Racial ideologies of Anglo-Saxon superiority could have also provoked Congressional and Supreme Court justice concerns about a territory's ability (intelligence and sophistication) to self-govern, which was the criterion for the endowment of statehood.

The reluctance of the US Congress to confer citizenship and execute a precise formula of incorporation demonstrates what appears to be a systematic denial of Constitutional rights to colored people—whether they were shades of black, brown, or yellow—within the American realm. Imperialists deliberately avoided mentioning race, while the national narrative hinged on racial ideologies, referencing social Darwinism, benevolent assimilation, the "white man's burden," and Anglo-Saxonism. African Americans also faced the continued denial of citizenship and other fundamental rights and privileges. In the 1830s, the Frenchman Alexis de Tocqueville wrote regarding the North:

> The electoral franchise has been conferred upon the Negroes in almost all States in which slavery has been abolished, but if they come forward to vote, their lives are in danger. If oppressed, they may bring action at law but they will find none but whites among their judges; and although they may serve

> legally as jurors, prejudice repels them from that office... The gates of heaven are not closed against them, but their inferiority is continued to the very confines of the other world... Thus the Negro is free [in the North,] but he can share neither the rights, nor the pleasures, nor the labor, nor the afflictions, nor the tomb of him whose equal he has been declared to be; and he cannot meet him upon fair terms in life nor in death. (de Tocqueville 2000, pp. 359–360)

Historian George Frederickson writes that racism should be recognized as much more than:

> an attitude or set of beliefs; it also expresses itself in practices, institutions, and structures that a sense of deep difference justifies or validates. Racism ... is more than theorizing about human differences or thinking badly of a group over which one has no control. It either directly sustains or proposes to establish a racial order, a permanent group hierarchy that is believed to reflect the laws and decrees of God. (Frederickson 2002, p. 24)[2]

The US Supreme Court only decided what Puerto Rico was *not*—it was not fully part of America but rather still a "forming part of America"—meaning that Puerto Ricans were Americans but not citizens, a decision that gave rise to their status as one of "domestic in a foreign sense" (Burnett and Marshall 2001; Bosniak 2008, pp. 2–6; Ngai 2005, p. 2).[3] An editorial describing the court's illogical determination rendered the situation nonsensical:

> Little by little the Porto Rican begins to find out where he stands and what he is. Not long ago his country was declared not to be a 'foreign country'; his ships are 'American'; as artist, he is 'American'; as sailor, he appears to be 'American'; and now it has been decided that he is not an 'alien.' In view of the [Court's] guarded statements, the almost total absence of discussion, and the fact that the question was *narrowed* to the interpretation of the word alien within the meaning of a particular act, it is difficult even to surmise the effect of this decision.[4]

The salience of race is the underlying difference between Puerto Rico and other insular territorial "Americans" and "continental Americans" after the Spanish-American War. Citizenship by birth has been the cornerstone to American democracy since the colonial days and was reaffirmed by the US Constitution (U.S. Const. amend. XIV, § 1). Traditionally, citizenship is secured by *jus soli* (birth on US soil) or by *jus sanguinis* (born to US citizen) or, secondarily, through the naturalization process (Wise 1997). Although the Constitution of 1789 included multiple provisions that addressed citizenship, it did not provide an exact definition, which allowed the process of determining citizenship to be applied less than equally.[5] In *Scott v. Sandford*, US Constitutional rights were only given to citizens within the American political community, and the US Supreme Court determined that "negroes" were categorized as "beings of an inferior order" and thus not part of the "people" as defined in the constitution (60 U.S. (19 How.) 393 (1857) (*Dred Scott*) at 411).[6] Each of these groups received "partial membership" in the American dominion. Partial membership is a political manifestation of the racial ideology consistent with the Supreme Court's earlier ruling *Plessy v. Ferguson* (1896) and systematic Chinese exclusionary mandates during the turn of the century.[7]

Some have suggested that the constructs of race played a role in the expressions of law, culture, religion, and politics in the newly Christianized islands of the South Pacific. Although I do not substantially address race within the political quagmire between the various federal and territorial bodies, race is politically and legally framed under the US Supreme Court's determination of outlying territories and its people. Race was the determining factor in deciding which territory would be considered a "desirable possession" based upon the ethnic makeup of the society (May 1968, pp. 100–101; Perea 2000, pp. 140–163). Expansionists argued for the acceptance of foreign "alien" mixtures in distant lands by appealing to the ideals implicit in the "white man's burden"—the more foreign, the more likely the blessings of American liberty and advancement would civilize and tame them. At the same time, the United States resisted claiming people of "too backward" a race that would threaten the makeup of the American political body. Paradoxically, the inclusion/exclusion scheme succeeds because it does not define the precise method for being classified as part of America. Without a precise method of inclusion, a "liminal space" is created that justifies racial discrimination and use race to determine when, who, and why people or lands are "desirable" (Kettner 2014; Lopez 2006). Resting on this racially discriminatory scheme of exclusion, the US Supreme Court in the insular cases has specified US Congress plenary power over the insular areas without limitations.

Organized, Unorganized, Unincorporated, Citizenship

Territory, narrowly identified by the pre-existing Northwest Territory at the time of the ratification of the Constitution, deemed as all non-state areas, which were typically wide-open spaces of land (Northwest Territory Ordinance of 1787, ch.8, 1 Stat. 50). Within the continental United States, territory classification had subdivisions: unincorporated or incorporated and organized or unorganized (Northwest Territory Ordinance of 1787, ch.8, 1 Stat. 50 § 6.5). A territory that does not have an Organic Act is defined as unorganized in US law. An Organic Act is an act of the US Congress that establishes a territory within the US body-politic or what can be labeled as being within the "domestic sphere."

American Sāmoa is one of five territories under the US flag. American Sāmoa, the Virgin Islands, and Guam are plainly known as territories. Puerto Rico and the Commonwealth of the Northern Mariana Islands (CNMI) are politically designated as commonwealths but legally classified as US territories. All five of the island territories are branded as "unincorporated" by the United States, because they are not inevitably destined to become states (Van Dyke 1992). All but American Sāmoa are considered "organized" because the US Congress has enacted an Organic Act to establish a civil government (Laughlin 1995). American Sāmoa is an anomaly. It is the only US territory that is politically and legally classified as "unorganized" and "unincorporated" because, although it has a legislature (*Fono*) and an elected governor, the operation of the civil government is not the result of an Organic Act (Román 2006, p. 184, 190; Laughlin 1984, p. 84). Without an Organic Act, the two ratified Deeds of Cession provide the US Congress with all governmental power over American Sāmoa under the US Constitution.

Guam and the Virgin Islands are organized territories under Organic Acts; their Constitutions may be changed by the people according to the terms within the Organic Act or by the US government. In the case of American Sāmoa, the "unorganized" status does not provide the benefits of being a more versatile governance structure because of the US Congress's bureaucratic layering of authorities. For example, revisions to the territorial American Sāmoa Constitution must be approved by the Secretary of the Interior and then ratified by an Act of Congress.[8]

US Supreme Court decisions dressed up exclusionary laws as "territorial doctrine," which masks the intent to protect the American political community and to prevent continental Americans from further inter-racial comingling.[9] Citizenship status of people living in insular territories is determined not through the US Constitution or the traditional birthright process to citizenship but rather through an Organic Act. Puerto Ricans received their US citizenship not through the Constitution but by the Jones Act of 1917, making them statutory citizens.[10]

In Guam, the Organic Act of 1950 established statutory US citizenship for its residents. People of the US Virgin Islands received statutory US citizenship in 1927. US Code also established start dates for each of these territories to determine when citizenship was conferred upon birth.[11] Federal Judge Juan R. Torruella criticizes the United States, "Court's repeated efforts to suppress these [citizenship] issues" with the stigma of inferiority:

> [W]e once more have before us issues that arise by reason of the political inequality that exists within the body politic of the United States, as regards the four million citizens of this Nation who reside in Puerto Rico [...] As in the case of racial segregation, see Plessy v. Ferguson, 163 U.S. 557 (1896) (overruled by Brown v. Bd. of Educ., 347 U.S. 482 (1954)), it is the courts that are responsible for the creation of this inequality. Furthermore, it is the courts that have clothed this noxious condition in a mantle of legal respectability. But perhaps even more egregious is the fact that it is this judiciary that has mechanically parroted the outdated and retrograde underpinnings on which this invented inferiority is perpetuated [...] Although the unequal treatment of persons because of the color of their skin or other irrelevant reasons, was then the modus operandi of governments, and an accepted practice of societies in general, the continued enforcement of these rules by the courts is today an outdated anachronism, to say the least. Such actions, particularly by courts of the United States, only serve to tarnish our judicial system as the standard-bearer of the best values to which our Nation aspires. Allowing these antiquated rules to remain in place, long after the unequal treatment of American citizens has become constitutionally, morally and culturally unacceptable in the rest of our Nation, see Brown v. Bd. of Educ., 347 U.S. 483, is an intolerable state of affairs which cannot be excused by hiding behind any theory of law [...] The suggestion that Appellants seek a political rather than a judicial remedy to correct the grievous violation of their rights claimed in this action, is, at a minimum, ironic given that it is precisely the lack of political representation that is the central issue in this case. It is this lack of any political power by these disenfranchised U.S. citizens, and the cat and mouse games that have been played with them by the United States government, including its

> courts, that have resulted in their interminable unequal condition. When this status of second-class citizenship is added to the also judicially established rule that grants Congress plenary powers over the territories and their inhabitants, i.e., that recognizes in Congress practically unfettered authority over the territories and their inhabitants, one has to ask what effective political process is the lead opinion suggesting be turned to by Appellants to resolve the constitutional issues raised by this case? In fact, the referral by the lead opinion to the exercise of political power by these disenfranchised citizens, as the solution to their political inequality is nothing more than the promotion of the continued colonial status that has existed since Puerto Rico was acquired by the United States as booty after the Spanish-American War of 1898. (*Gregorio Igartúa et. al v. United States of America et. al.* No.09-2189, United States Court of Appeals, First Circ. (Nov. 24, 2010))

Citizenship status allocates not just rights, privileges, and recognition but also "notions of membership, representation, or political participation" to an individual within the US sphere while concurrently situating their place within the American political community (Sparrow 2006, p. 161). Chief Justice William Rehnquist has affirmatively declared, "In constitutionally defining who is a citizen of the United States, Congress obviously thought it was doing something, and something important. Citizenship meant something, a status in and relationship with a society which is continuing and more basic than mere presence or residence" (*Sugarman v. Dougall*, 413 U.S. 634, 652 (1973)). Law professor Ediberto Román describes it:

> Citizenship, therefore, involves more than the right 'to go to the seat of government;' it also includes the sense of permanent inclusion in the American political community in a non-subordinate condition, in contrast to the position of aliens. The label 'citizen' is applicable only to a person who is endowed with full political and civil rights in the body politic of the state. Thus, citizenship signifies an individual's 'full membership' in a political community where the ideal of equality is supposed to prevail. (Román 1998)

Classically, the Western concept of citizen can be traced to Aristotle in the mid-300 BC. Aristotle claimed that "a state is composite, like any other whole made up of many parts; these are the citizens, who compose it" (Aristotle 2004, p. 126). Upon drafting the US Constitution, the founding fathers found it important to address the need to protect the citizenry. James Madison writes in Federalist Paper No. 51:

> Different interests necessarily exist in different classes of citizens. If a majority be united by a common interest, the rights of the minority will be insecure. There are but two methods of providing against this evil: the one by creating a will in the community independent of the majority, that is, of the society itself; the other by comprehending in the society so many separate descriptions of citizens, as will render an unjust combination of a majority of the whole improbable, if not impracticable. (Rossiter 1961, pp. 323–324)

The Fourteenth Amendment to the US Constitution details the provision for citizenship: "All persons born and naturalized in the United States, and subject to the jurisdiction thereof, are citizens of the United States and the state wherein they reside" (U.S. Const. art. XIV, § 2). The Fourteenth Amendment affirms that some places that are not "within" the United States are still subject to its authority. Birthright citizenship under the Citizenship Clause, however, "is not extended" to persons born in US territories.[12]

US Citizenship and American Sāmoa

Cynics may argue that, relative to the full membership and equality that continental Americans enjoy, the law has created an inferior citizenship for insular "noncitizen Nationals" and "statutory granted citizens" (Bender 2006, p. 222; Smith 2001, pp. 373–386; Thornbugh 2001, pp. 349–371). In American Sāmoa's case, "partial membership" works to protect the customary institutions and traditions, and so a push for full equality is not readily embraced by the American Sāmoa citizenry. Full application of the US Constitution would unravel the existing protections for communal land tenure, which is founded upon race and the chiefly (nobility) title system.

In addition to civil and human rights, the following individual rights are enumerated in the Revised Constitution of American Sāmoa, Article I: "separating church and state; freedom of press, religion, speech, and assembly; right to petition the government for redress of grievances, due process prohibits the deprivation of life, liberty, or property without due process of law and requires just compensation when private property is taken for public use" (Ntumy et al. 1993, p. 442). Certain provisions of the US Bill of Rights also provide for individual rights: the dignity of the individual to be respected, that a person is presumed innocent until pronounced guilty by law, the privilege of the writ of habeas corpus, and the prohibition of cruel or unusual punishments (Ntumy et al. 1993, p. 443). In American Sāmoa the enumeration of human and individual rights within the revised constitution also supports and identifies the customary traditions of the *fa'asāmoa*, namely, customary land.

American Sāmoans = US Nationals

American Sāmoans are US nationals and not US citizens (8 U.S.C. § 1101 (22) (b)). US nationals cannot vote for the US president, but they may work and live anywhere in the United States, they are eligible to apply for a US passport, and they may apply for US citizenship through the naturalization process. The Revised Constitution of American Sāmoa provides Constitutional protections to native American Sāmoans against alienation of lands and protections against the destruction of the Sāmoan way of life (Revised Constitution of American Sāmoa, art. I, § 3; *Craddick v. Territorial Registrar*, 1 A.S.R.2d 10 (1980)). US citizenship, however, is derived from the Fourteenth Amendment to the US Constitution or would originate from a specific statute signed into law by the US Congress to confer citizenship. Statutory citizenship has been enacted for every other insular territory, including Puerto Rico, CNMI, Guam, and Virgin Islands (8 U.S.C. § 1407; 8 U.S.C. § 1406).

US nationals may obtain US citizenship via naturalization; if they have lived in any outlying US territory for a minimum of five years immediately preceding their application, they can become citizens by moving to continental America and establishing domicile there for at least three months (8 U.S.C. § 1436, 8 U.S.C. § 1427).

There is one exception to this rule. Any US national or alien who was on reserve or on active-duty status in the Armed Forces during hostility periods designated by the President through Executive Order—including World War I, World War II, Korean and Vietnam hostilities—and who was engaged in armed conflict with foreign forces, may receive immediate citizenship under the special wartime provision (8 U.S.C. § 1440; 8 C.F.R. 329.2). For American Sāmoan soldiers, this special wartime provision was first used on September 10, 2010, when 42 Toa o Sāmoa soldiers were sworn in as US citizens by the US Citizenship and Immigration Services (USCIS) ("Am. Samoa Soldiers" 2015). Several dozen American Sāmoa

If the CAC lawsuit were successful and the federal courts mandated automatic citizenship in American Sāmoa based on the Fourteenth Amendment and the citizenship clause, then the equal protection and due process clauses would also come into play. American Sāmoa currently practices American Sāmoan-only land ownership and the *fa'asāmoa mātai* system that is incorporated into the *Fono,* a bi-cameral legislature. In the Senate, "only a registered *mātai* of a Sāmoan family who fulfills his obligations as required by Sāmoan custom in the county from which he is elected may be a Senator" (A.S.C.A. § 2.0203 et seq. (1968)). Additionally, "Senators must be elected in accordance with Sāmoan custom by the County Councils of the County or Counties they are to represent" (A.S.C.A. § 2.0203 et seq. (1968)). American Sāmoa currently violates the equal protection and due process clauses of the Fourteenth Amendment by practicing ethnicity-based land ownership, adhering to a nobility system (*mātai*), and following an election process that requires of civil servants to the Senate performance of *chiefly* custom. No other American state has ethnicity-based exclusionary laws and practices that require title and cultural performance for elected officials. If the citizenship clause is mandated, American Sāmoa will not be allowed to continue with these "unconstitutional," traditional cultural practices.

During the time that this case was still active, there was concern that a federal court halfway around the world could have unilaterally applied the Fourteenth Amendment, in its entirety, to American Sāmoa. Delegate Faleomavaega argued that this citizenship issue must be decided by local American Sāmoa US nationals, not by any overseas entity attempting to circumvent the local political process, including the federal courts in Washington DC. US Department of the Interior Assistant Secretary Eileen Sobeck testified before the US Senate Committee on Energy and Natural Resources regarding Senate Bill 1237, the Omnibus Territories Act of 2013, on July 11, 2013 in the 113th US Congress (S. 1237 Omnibus Territories Act 2013). Sobeck recognized the US national status reserved for persons born in American Sāmoa, which was upheld on June 26, 2013, by the United States District Court for the District of Columbia (*Leneuoti Fiafia Tuaua* et al. *v. United States,* et al., 951 F. Supp. 2d. 88 (D.C. Cir. 2013)). Sobeck states that "To date, the Congress has not seen fit to bestow birthright citizenship on American Sāmoa, and in accordance with the law, this Court must and will respect that choice" (S. 1237 Omnibus Territories Act of 2013; *Tuaua v. United States,* 951 F. Supp. 2d. 88 (D.C. Cir. 2013)). Sobeck went on to say that the plebiscite called for in section 19 of the Omnibus Act will bring new discussion and a collective vote in American Sāmoa if the people favor citizenship. The formal procedure vis-à-vis the US Congress should first be met domestically, through the democratic process of voting by residents who live in the territory to determine if they favor birthright citizenship. If so, then American Sāmoa leaders can approach the Secretary of the Interior and the US Congress to seek action on the citizenship issue.

It is political naiveté to think that the federal courts will agree to apply the Fourteenth Amendment selectively to protect American Sāmoan customs and traditions. Although the CAC lawsuit may only address the citizenship clause now, the outcome of this lawsuit may demand the full application of the Fourteenth Amendment, including due process and equal protection, in American Sāmoa.

US Department of the Interior

It is critical to note that the Secretary of the Interior and the US Congress have granted American Sāmoa constitutionally protected provisions of custom and tradition. In February 19, 1951, President Harry Truman sent a letter to the Department of the Interior about its new role in administering American Sāmoa (replacing the Naval Administration). The letter states, "In particular, I want the people of Sāmoa to have my personal assurance that their traditional rights and lands will be protected while, with their help, the civilian administration finds ways to promote their political, economic, and educational advancement" (Pacific Island Reports 1950, pp. 61–65). In 1960, the Department of the Interior issued a special policy statement on American Sāmoa and the need to protect the culture. It proclaims:

> [T]he political structure of the government shall be in accord with the desires of the Sāmoan people in regard to such adaptations as may be desirable by virtue of Sāmoan customs, traditions and land ownership. During the period of development of self-government, the people and their resources shall be protected against undesirable exploitation. Protection of Sāmoans against the loss of their family lands is an important policy not only as regards the economy, but also as it may affect the Sāmoan '*mātai*' system. It is the policy to maintain this protection. (Annual Report of the Governor of American Samoa to the Secretary of the Interior. 1960. Report [Appendix III, State of Objectives and Policies], p.71)

The retention of Sāmoan cultural identity is further articulated in the American Sāmoa Constitution of 1960 and American Sāmoa Code

Annotated (Revised Constitution of American Samoa, art. I §3; A.S.C.A. 1.0202). The "partial membership" of American Sāmoa in the American body-politic, by virtue of its definition by the US Supreme Court as an unorganized and unincorporated territory, tolerates these cultural protections within the US sphere of influence, as long as the US federal courts do not decide otherwise.

American Sāmoa Today

Society

Prior to the influence of Western nations, the Sāmoan Islands included both the Independent State of Sāmoa and the eastern islands, now known as American Sāmoa. For over 3000 years, the Sāmoan isles were independently ruled by the *fa'amatai* system. The *mātais* are part of a complex social and political system of chiefly title holders of rank. It was and is not common for these titled rankings to be realigned as land for ownership and other natural resources are exchanged and as the *mātais* engage in conflict and war among themselves (Sunia 1988). The Sāmoans' adaptation of Western lifestyles, governance systems, and the English language proves that even though the *fa'asāmoa* allows for changes, the foundation remains: *āiga, mātai* system, and communal lands. American Sāmoa has adopted the English language as the official language in the territory, has accepted strong Christian influence, and has an American-style government and education system. Family members offer monetary donations to assist family during *fa'alavelaves*[14] (church and family-related events). The Western system of currency and monetary exchange is now very much part of the Sāmoan custom.

Before the mid-1970s, most American Sāmoans relied primarily on traditional subsistence fishing and agriculture. Once modern (Western) self-governance took form, the moneyed economy slowly replaced subsistence living and lifestyle. The first major milestone toward territorial self-governance was the adoption of the first constitution in 1960. However, self-governance in any insular territory is not absolute because the territorial constitution, popular elections, and local governing authority are granted at the discretion of the US Secretary of the Interior (Exec. Order No. 10264, 3 C.F.R., 1949–1953).

Before 1977, all Governors and Lieutenant Governors in American Sāmoa were appointed. Between 1900 and 1951, the US Department of

State appointed these posts then from 1951 to 1976 the US Secretary of the Interior took over administration of appointees. In the mid-1970s, a serious push for more local autonomy motivated the *Fono* to initiate the creation of American Sāmoa Public Law 13-23, which put into place procedures to elect the Governor and Lieutenant Governor. With approval and consent of the appointed Governor of American Sāmoa, a request was sent to the US Secretary of the Interior for a Secretarial Order that would provide authority for the popular election of the Governor and Lieutenant Governor. The request was approved on September 13, 1977 (Exec. Order No. 10264, 3 C.F.R., 1949–1953). General elections for the first elected Governor and Lieutenant Governor began in January 1978 (A.S.C.A. §41.0302 et seq. (1984)). In the summer of 1978, the *Fono* of American Sāmoa further requested the Attorney General be appointed by the elected Governor and subject to confirmation by the *Fono* (3 A.S.C. 12(c); P.L. 15-23 1978). The Secretary of the Interior approved this request as well. Between 1900 and 1951, the Secretary of the Navy appointed High Court judges. During this time, the President of the High Court were solely US Navy Officers, while the District Judge for most of all the early cases was Edwin W. Gurr, and the District Judge for the Sāmoan political districts was an appointed senior *mātai*.[15] During the infancy of this US territory, without formal experience in imperialistic expansionism, there was no existing framework of federal-to-outpost governance to implement in American Sāmoa. Due to the archipelago's remote geographic location and a slow, boat-driven mail system, the US Navy Officers stationed in Pago Pago had complete and nearly autonomous power and authority in the islands. There was no master plan for the territory, other than to build a naval coaling station and create a solid American presence in the "South Seas."

This system continued until the 1960s, when the social and economic infrastructure of the territory grew. As a nod to American Sāmoa, President John F. Kennedy appointed Governor John Hayden to expedite Sāmoan development. During the 1960s a new hospital, roads, public schools, and television transmission facilities were constructed. American Sāmoa was transformed into a modern island economy with the requisite infrastructure to secure private sector growth.

By the mid-1970s, the population and economy of American Sāmoa industrialized at approximately 2.7 percent annually, driven in part by the establishment of the Starkist Sāmoa cannery in Pago Pago harbor. The tuna industry is the backbone of the economy of American Sāmoa. The

United States got tariff-free access to tuna canned in American Sāmoa, and qualifying US corporations investing in American Sāmoa got reduced federal taxes on income earned there (26 U.S.C. §936, 26 U.S.C. §30A note). Incentives for foreign investment in American Sāmoa established by the US Internal Revenue Code provided the vehicle for private sector growth, which led to an expansion of supplier businesses to accommodate the tuna industry's growth.

Population Demographics

The estimated population in American Sāmoa is 62,117. High fertility and high immigration drive the population structure. The local-born population has been dwarfed by the immigrant population, most of whom come from Sāmoa, other Pacific Islands, and Asia, principally to work in the canneries. Despite the political divide between Sāmoa and American Sāmoa, their linguistic and cultural ties remain strong due to *fa'asāmoa*, *mātai* titles, and communal lands.

Since the 1950s, immigrant Sāmoans from Sāmoa flocked to the shores of American Sāmoa for US currency and employment opportunities with higher pay. Moreover, American entitlement programs are a significant pull for families who gain access to the federal school lunch program, Women and Infant Children's (WIC) supplemental food vouchers, a free public-school system, and subsidized health care system not available in independent Sāmoa. Between 1920 and 1970, population growth rates were extraordinary in American Sāmoa. In 1920, the population was 8056 people, which grew 24.7 percent in the next decade. By 1940, the population had increased another 28.4 percent, then 46.7 percent by 1950, 5.9 percent by 1960, and 35.5 percent by 1970 (Park 1972). At least 30 percent of the total population left American Sāmoa's borders in the 1950s, but growth continued, in large part due to the ineffective immigration management, port-of-entry control, and a lack of government database system to monitor people who overstayed. As an unincorporated territory, American Sāmoa is the only US territory that still regulates its own customs and immigration. The problem areas listed above were reported in the 2000 Governor Togiola Tulafono Task Force on Population Growth, which also cautioned that in 2000, with 48 percent of the population under the age of 20 years, population growth would continue for at least another generation ("Impacts of Rapid Population" 2000).

The patterns of migration reveal the inflow of Sāmoans into American Sāmoa for employment and higher minimum wages in US currency and the outflow of American Sāmoans to continental America for military service, education, higher wages, and access to American amenities. Migration from Sāmoa to American Sāmoa is a relatively easy transition, as the shared language, food, religion, dress, traditions and spiritual beliefs, gender roles, and everyday patterns of daily life activities are the same or very similar between the two jurisdictions. Physically they are separated by a 20-minute flight or a six- to eight-hour ferry, on the *Lady Naomi* vessel. Migration rates, both in and out, are largely influenced by the economic and employment opportunities in the territory. The migration patterns for American Sāmoa are quite difficult to forecast due to many factors, including poor computer systems for immigration and customs and immigration sponsorship schemes that leave many illegal overstayers jumping from sponsor to sponsor. Most importantly, the federal government's unpredictable formula for determining federal minimum wage amounts and implementation dates, the changing restrictions on financial entitlement programs and grants, and investment caps on industries for all territories strongly influence migration.

In 2000, the median age for males was 21, as opposed to 21.7 for females, which reflects higher male mortality and the expected rise in aged dependency with the higher median age of the population. From 1950 to 2010, the median age rose progressively from 17.7 years in 1960 to 21.3 years in 2000.

The overall population of American Sāmoa has more than doubled from 1970 to 2010 from 27,000 residents in 1970 to 57,000 net residents in 2010. American Sāmoa's rate of natural increase remained high between 2000 and 2010, due mostly to the large base of young adults and its positive impact on birth rates. Noticeable increases occurred during the 1980s when the tuna industries recruited foreign workers, and the upsurge in net migration in the 2000s demonstrates the high depletion of residents and the lowered inflow of foreign workers. Retaining a skilled and educated workforce is dependent on a stable and flourishing economy, and the tuna industry has remained the only stable industry in American Sāmoa. Given that the US Congress has ultimate plenary powers over all territories, and that the myriad of federal laws are variably applicable across the territories, each territory faces an uphill battle to secure private sector incentives.

The population growth can be divided into two growth periods: the first under traditional subsistence up until the mid-1970s, and the second under a modern economy from the mid-1970s to present. Infrastructural and educational development began when governance over American Sāmoa transferred from the Navy to the Department of the Interior in 1951 (16 Fed. Reg. 6419 (1951); 48 U.S.C. § 1661 (c)). Until 1951, US Naval Officers served as Governors. Governance over American Sāmoa by the Secretary of the Interior was done through the appointments of Governor, Lieutenant Governor, Chief Justice, Associate Justices, Attorney General, and other governmental offices. The ultimate responsibility for the administration of the Territory rested and continues to reside in the Secretary of the Interior.

US Possessions, Not Territories

US possessions are atolls, coral reefs, national marine monuments, and wildlife island refuge sites that do not have permanent human populations. The temporary residents are scientists and military personnel who do not need to seek self-determination or self-governance. In 2015, the US possessions classified are Baker, Howland, Kingman Reef, Jarvis, Midway, Palmyra, Wake, and Johnston Islands. Of these, Palmyra Atoll is owned by the Nature Conservancy; Wake Island is an unincorporated territory of the United States that is administered by the Department of the Interior and the US Air Force (Department of Defense); and Johnston Atoll is managed by the Department of Defense. All except Wake and Johnston Islands are administered as National Wildlife Refuges (NWR) by the US Fish and Wildlife Service of the Department of the Interior.

Imprecise Territorial Framework

The Executive Branch affirmed that the US Congress has plenary powers over the territories. Between 1898 and 1917, the Judicial Branch established the framework in which the Territorial doctrine is structured. Between 1925 and 1974, the Supreme Court withdrew from hearing territorial status cases, and post-1974 judicial rulings have favored decisive plenary powers of the US Congress over the territories.[16] Territories have each taken individualized approaches toward lobbying for US citizenship, increased federal government support and awareness, increased local autonomy, and economic and trade free from fetters of the US Department of State. The US Constitution offers very little direction by way of express wording about territorial expansion. The US Congress's power to admit new states and its authority over territory and lands are articulated in the US Constitution Article IV Sections 2 and 3. American expansionism into the Pacific was about military and economic power. The Naval coaling station in Tutuila gave the US power to intercede in international trade and insert strategic military outposts for commerce and warfare. Land was essential to American growth and was obtained beginning with the 1783 Treaty of Paris and followed by the purchase of the Louisiana territory; the acquisition of California, Nevada, Utah, and parts of Wyoming, Colorado, New Mexico, and Arizona (also known as the Mexican Cession) and the acquisition of Alaska provided the early stages of US government absorption of new lands into the American body-politic (Onuf 1987; Pomeroy 1969; Weinberg 1963; Bestor 1973, pp. 10–50). These early continental lands were formally organized and made into US territories with the presumption of eventual membership in the Union.

The Spanish-American War of 1898 marked the beginning of a new breed of "unincorporated territories," territories without express predisposition toward statehood or sovereignty that were subject to different treatment within the US empire. The continual confusion of privileges and benefits versus rights and mandates when analyzing territories, their land issues, territorial policy, and federal mandates requires a closer examination of each territory's evolution toward or away from the United States.

Philippines, Puerto Rico, and Guam: Unincorporated Classification of US Territories

The unincorporated territorial classification was decidedly useful to the national government looking for ways to handle "terminally backward societies" of foreign islands. The unincorporated status allowed the United States to claim it was pursuing democracy for "former" colonies, while creating a slippery slope of potential legal and ethical responsibilities. The Philippines and its people were handled differently than the Northwest colonies, for example, because the former were not incorporated into the US body-politic. Unincorporated status given to US territories allowed for only fundamental rights apply as a matter of law, while non-fundamental rights were not granted. This judicially created phraseology delineates rights and privileges to legitimize the American imperialist formula without bilaterally consenting to US citizenship or other Constitutional rights. "Unincorporated" territorial status is a de facto classification that allows the US Congress to determine the rights and privileges of territorial residents depending on the extent that each outpost can be considered "international" or "domestic" (US GAO 1997, p. 24).

The United States did not have centuries of experiences with empire building, as did the Spaniards or Portuguese who had many colonial settlements throughout the world. Rather, 1898 marked a new horizon for the relatively young America. The political legitimacy of absorbing the Philippines Islands as a territory into the American body-politic was achieved through propaganda promoting economic interests in Asia. US foreign policy at that time attempted to draw a distinction between the old and new worlds. The United States wanted to support Latin and South American countries' efforts to gain independence from Spain and Portugal. In the early nineteenth century, the Monroe Doctrine attempted to create distinct European and American spheres of influence; the United States saw expansion into this southern region to gain international influence.

Philippines

Before the turn of the twentieth century, US President William McKinley's Benevolent Assimilation Proclamation espoused the American duty to civilize, educate, and improve the social condition of Filipinos. The Philippines was an American project of imperialistic territorial acquisition and served as naval support base located between the Pacific and South China Sea. This military position facilitated strategic US shipping lines to the Southeastern Asian trading markets of China, Indonesia, and Japan (Laughlin 1996, pp. 675–678).

At the close of the 1898 Treaty of Paris, the United States paid $20 million to Spain in exchange for its ceding the Philippines, Cuba, and Guam to America (Miller 1982). However, the 1899–1902 Philippine Insurrection, or what is known in the United States as the Philippine-American War, was a continuation of the Filipinos' fight for freedom, formerly from Spain and this time from the United States Filipinos believed that independence would be granted after the 1898 Spanish War. At the signing of the Treaty of Paris, though, no Filipinos, Sāmoans, or representatives from any other indigenous group were permitted access to the negotiation table where their lands were carved up and traded.

In 1892, during Spanish colonial rule, La Liga Filipina society was established as a peaceful mutual aid organization to present economic and social reforms to the colonial rulers in the Spanish Cortes (Parliament)

(O'Gorman 2005, pp. 129–150). La Liga Filipina set out to unite all Filipinos across the archipelago against the cruelties of Spanish rule, to educate Filipinos on commerce by way of agricultural techniques, and, most importantly, to create unity throughout the Philippine archipelago (O'Gorman 2005). The Spanish Cortes became alarmed by the growing membership of the pro-Filipino La Liga and sought to dismantle it, in part by arresting La Liga Filipina's leader, Dr. José Rizal (O'Gorman 2005). Andres Bonifacio, one of the founding members of the La Liga Filipina, was so moved by the reformist ideals that in 1892 he established the Kataas-taasan, Kagalang-galangang Katipunan ng̃ mg̃á Anak ng̃ Bayan, also known as "Katipunan," a militant anti-Spanish secret society. Katipunan continued to organize Filipinos in provinces throughout the Philippine archipelago and prepared them to win their country's independence by armed revolution (O'Gorman 2005, pp. 150–170). In 1896, the Katipunan openly encouraged a nationwide armed revolution against the Spanish by initiating multiple revolts in neighboring provinces with minor victories that culminated in Bonifacio's execution in 1897 (O'Gorman 2005).

Plunging the American flag into Filipino soil was successful only through the allied resistance to Spain by militant pro-independent Filipino groups like the Katipunan. Unsurprisingly, the exiting Spanish and the entering United States did not recognize Emilio Aguinaldo as the President of the First Philippine Republic at the close of the Spanish-American War because he sought to create a politically engaged populace (O'Gorman 2005). Democracy was a catchphrase used to promote an American-styled nationalistic ideology of dominance. Filipinos who once fought alongside US soldiers against the Spaniards were now considered insurgents, bandits who fought against "civilization and progress." The Philippines remained an unincorporated and unorganized territory for 37 years, from Spain's exit until it achieved Commonwealth status in 1935. The Philippines was considered to be a foreign and brutish backward people without civility or the capability to uphold democratic principles, stranding them in an unincorporated territorial status for their entire time under the US flag.

Puerto Rico and Guam

Puerto Rico and Guam's political and legal status was mostly dictated through the US Congress and insular cases (US Supreme Court). Unlike the Philippines, the unincorporated status of Puerto Rico and Guam had been fueled by territorial-to-federal politicking, ultimately working toward commonwealth status and greater self-autonomy. Under international law, the United States acquired these lands by occupation, since they were not already part of a state and cession of land by a treaty (August 1995). All islands ceded to the US were placed under military governments directly under the US Department of Defense.

US economic and military interests in Puerto Rico were designed to fortify the proposed canal across the isthmus of Central America, and Guam was the Pacific Island naval position for defense purposes and international trade. The 1900 Organic Act for Puerto Rico and 1950 Organic Act of Guam were ambiguous in addressing their foreign/domestic status and created confusion regarding federal taxes on their exports to America. Puerto Ricans were experts at working political parties and western politics, having survived under Spanish rule for over three centuries (Wells 1971, pp. 126–128).

The 1900 Organic Act or Foraker Act, for Puerto Rico, was hugely important for the newly inducted US territory. The act granted Puerto Rico a limited government that was both civilian and elected by the populace (Public Law 56-191, 31 Stat.77, April 2, 1900). US birthright citizenship was specifically withheld from Puerto Rico (Treaty of Paris, Dec. 10, 1898, art. IX, 39 Stat. 1754, 1759 (1899)). Guam's 1950 Organic Act provided the territory with similar measures of limited self-governance, but most importantly, Guam's residents were granted US birthright citizenship (48 U.S.C. § 1421). Both Organic Acts politically organized the territories, changing their status from unorganized to organized.

Although the Organic Acts made these territories politically "organized," all organized and unorganized territories were and are still subject to the Congress's plenary powers under the US Constitution Territorial Clause (U.S. Const. art. IV, § 3). The second Organic Act, or the Jones-Shafroth Act of 1917, granted for Puerto Ricans US birthright citizenship and made all federal laws applicable to Puerto Rico, while at the same time designating Puerto Rican exports as "foreign" (Leech 1959, pp. 487–503). Even as Puerto Rico was becoming more closely aligned to full statehood with popular elections, civilian government, and US birthright citizenship, its unincorporated classification allowed the United States to treat the territory as a foreign country in matters of trade. The tariffs imposed on Puerto Rico's main export commodities such as coffee, sugar, and tobacco were disastrous to its economy. Federal taxes on Puerto Rican exports, which led to various insular cases over Puerto Rico, complicated the US government's administration of the territory, both because of the amount of revenue that was being generated and the precedent that these cases set for other territories.

The United States instigated, through Puerto Rico and Guam, a precedent for how unincorporated and organized territories can be treated as American and foreign countries at the same time (*Rassmussen v. United States,* 197 U.S. 516 (1905)). The evolution of policy in the US Congress and US Supreme Court law allows each branch of government to define a territory as domestically American while simultaneously foreign in certain aspects. The US Supreme Court manufactured a trivial legal justification for this "domestic and foreign" treatment in *Balzac v. People of Puerto Rico*:

> Alaska was a very different case from that of Porto [sic] Rico. It was an enormous territory, very sparsely settled and offering opportunity for immigration and settlement by American citizens. It was on the American continent and within easy reach of the United States. It involved none of the difficulties which incorporation of the Philippines and Porto [sic] Rico presents. (258 U.S. 289, 309 (1922))

Constitutional law professor Efrén Rivera Ramos points out that there are benefits to being treated as a foreign territory while also having access to US citizenship, the primary one being political flexibility. Still, Ramos reminds us, colonialism has never been a unidimensional phenomenon over time without caveats of promise and demise (Ramos 2001, p. 109). Ramos concedes the unlimited power the US government exercises over these unincorporated territories does not conform to democratic ideals, and he compares this American legalistic maneuvering to colonialism (Ramos 2001, p. 109).

Notes

1. Justice Brown described territorial residents as "alien races" in *Downes v. Bidwell,* 182 US 244, 287, 45 L.Ed. 1088, 21 S. Ct. 770 (1901), the leading insular case. For more on race and annexation, see Josê Cabranes, *Citizenship and the American Empire,* 178 U. Pa. L. Rev. 391 at 421 & n. 104 (1978). Racism was a crucial factor in congressional debates regarding annexation of insular territories (Bender 2006, 190).
2. George Frederickson, *Racism, A Short Story* (Princeton: Princeton University Press, 2002), 24; Barbara J. Fields, "Slavery, Race and Ideology

in the United States of America," *New Left Review* 1, no. 181 (May/June 1990); Eric T. Love, *Race over Empire: Racism and U.S. Imperialism 1865–1900* (Chapel Hill: University of North Carolina Press, 2004); Peter J. Spiro, *Beyond Citizenship: American Identity after Globalization* (New York: Oxford University Press, 2008).

3. *Foreign in a Domestic Sense: Puerto Rico, American Expansion, and the Constitution*, eds. Christina D. Burnett and Burke Marshall (Durham: Duke University Press, 2000). In light of the US Supreme Court's resistance to the idea of an "American alien," it is worth noting that scholars of citizenship studies have recently coined the phrase "alien citizens" to capture the relationship between exclusionary and inclusionary policies in American political membership. For more detail on ideas of citizenship that helped me to situate American Sāmoa and citizenship, see Linda Bosniak, *The Citizen and the Alien: Dilemmas of Contemporary Membership* (Princeton: Princeton University Press, 2008), 2–6; Ngai, *Impossible Subjects*, 2.
4. Quoted in Christina Duffy Burnett, "'They say I am not an American…' The Noncitizen National and the Law of American Empire," in *Virginia Journal of International Law* 48, no. 4 (2009), 708.
5. US Const. art. I, § 2, cl. 2: (a member of the House of Representatives must have been "a Citizen of the United States" for seven years); US Const. art. I § 3, cl. 3: (a senator must have been "a Citizen of the United States" for nine years), Act of March 26, 1790, ch. 3, § 1, 1 Stat. 103, 103–04 [repealed 1795] (A "free white person" could apply for citizenship after two years of residency in the United States).
6. Subsequent US Supreme Court decisions attempted to rectify this wrong to the definition of citizenship by the enactment of the 1868 Fourteenth Amendment that meant to protect people of all races.
7. In *Plessy v. Ferguson*, 163 U.S. 537 (1896) the US Supreme Court held that the "separate but equal" provision of private services mandated by state government is constitutional under the Equal Protection Clause of the US Constitution. The "separate but equal" doctrine was frequently used by courts of law until *Brown v. Board of Education* [347 U.S. 483 (1954)], when it was repudiated as unconstitutional. *Chae Chan Ping v. US*, 130 US 581 [1889]) held that the Congressional Act of 1888 which prohibited Chinese laborer from entering the United States who had departed before its passage, Chae Chan Ping was excluded for those reasons even with a certificate of reentry; court held that the US has the right to exclude foreigners at any time. For exclusionary Chinese citizenship laws and the associated policies, see Ngai (2005), pp. 40–59; Lee (2007); General citizenship and race see James Kettner (1978) The Development of American Citizenship 1608–1870 (Chapel Hill: University of North Carolina Press).

8. See Congressional Act December 8, 1983, P.L. 98–213, Sec. 12 97 Stat. 1462 (1983), 48 USCS § 1662a (1993) "Amendments of, or modifications to, the Constitution of American Sāmoa, as approved by the Secretary of the Interior pursuant to Executive Order 10264 [unclassified] as in effect January 1, 1983, may be made only by Act of Congress."
9. Puerto Rico is the best example of a territory that was unwanted as a state due to its racial composition and non-English-speaking native population.
10. Ch. 145, 39 Stat. 951, 953 (1917) (codified as amended in scattered sections of 48 USC). Statutory citizenship continues under 8 USC § 1402 (1994).
11. Guam Organic Act of 1950, 48 USC §1421. For more about citizenship at birth after 1949, see 8 USC § 1408, *The Statutes at Large of the United State of America. from December 1, 1925 to March 1927* (Washington, DC: U.S. Government Printing Office, 1927), XLiV, part 2, (1927):1234–1235; 8 U.S.C. 1406.
12. US Const. art. XIV, § 2.; *Valmonte v. INS,* 136 F.3d 914, 920 (2d Cir. 1998); *Lacap v. INS,* 138 F. 3d 518, 519 (3d Cir. 1998); *Licudine v. Winder*, 603 F. Supp. 2d 129 (D.D.C. 2009).
13. American Sāmoa Bar Association Law Conference, American Sāmoa Community College Conference Room, April 28th, 2012; Fainu´ulelei Alailima-Utu, Charles Alailima, Roy Hall, Afoa L. Suesue Lutu (Panelists without papers [all panelists are Sāmoan and practicing attorneys in American Sāmoa]).
14. *Fa'alavelaves* are cultural and family-related events that require family members to contribute money and/or commodity items (fine mats) for weddings, funerals, *mātai* titles, and church activities. These events also provide financial assistance for basic family needs.
15. US Department of Navy General Order No. 540 (February 19, 1900) reads in part: "In accordance with the foregoing, the Islands of Tutuila, of the Sāmoan Group, and all other islands of the group east of Longitude 171 degrees west of Greenwich, are hereby established into a Naval Station to be known as the Naval Station, Tutuila, and to be under the command of a Commandant." The first Commandant over the United States Navy Service in American Sāmoa was Commandant Benjamin F. Tilley. Attorney Edwin Gurr was also the author of the two Tutuila and Manu'a Deeds of Cession.
16. *Fornaris v. Ridge Tool Co.*, 400 US 41 (1970); *Guam v. Olson,* 431 US 195 (1977); *Sakamoto v. Duty Free Shoppers, Ltd.*, 764 F.2d 1285 (9th Cir. 1985).

References

"Am. Sāmoa Soldiers To Become Naturalized U.S. Citizens." *Sāmoa News*, October 5, 2015.

Balzac v. Porto Rico, 258 U.S. 298, 66 L. Ed. 627, 42 S. Ct. 343 (1922).

Craddick v. Territorial Registrar, 1 A.S.R. 2d 10 (1980).

Gregorio Igartúa et al. v. United States of America et al. No.09-2189, United States Court of Appeals, First Circ., (Nov. 24, 2010).

Leneuoti Fiafia Tuaua et al. v. United States, et al., 951 F. Supp. 2d. 88 (D.C. Cir. 2013).

Leneuoti Fiafia Tuaua, et al. v. United States of America, et al., No.15981 (2016).

Rassmussen v. United States, 197 U.S. 516 (1905).

Scott vs. Sandford (60 U.S. (19 How.) 393 (1857) (*Dred Scott*).

Sugarman v. Dougall, 413 U.S. 634, 652 (1973) (Rehnquist, J. dissenting).

A.S.C.A. § 1.0202 (1961).

A.S.C.A. § 2.0203 (1968).

A.S.C.A. §41.0302 (1984).

3 A.S.C. 12(c); P.L. 15-23, Secretary's Order No.3009 Amendment No.2, June 27, 1978.

8 U.S.C. § 1406.

8 U.S.C. § 1407.

8 U.S.C. § 1427.

8 U.S.C. § 1436.

26 U.S.C. §936, 26 U.S.C. §30A note.

48 U.S.C. § 1421.

U.S. Const. art. I, § 8.

U.S. Const. art. IV, § 3, cl. 3.

U.S. Const. amend. XIV, § 1.

U.S. Const. amend. XIV, § 1-5.

U.S. Const. art. XIV, § 2.

8 U.S.C. § 1101(2)(b).

8 U.S.C. § 1440; 8 C.F.R. 329.2, 1406.

Public Law 56-191, 31 Stat.77, April 2, 1900.

Rossiter, Clinton, ed. 1961. *The Federalist Papers*. New York: Penguin Books.

Annual Report of the Governor of American Samoa to the Secretary of the Interior. 1960. Report [Appendix III, State of Objectives and Policies].

Aristotle. 2004. 350 B.C.E. *Politics*. Books III 126.

Bender, Thomas. 2006. *A Nation Among Nations: America's Place in World History*. New York: Hill and Wang.

Bestor, Arthur. 1973. Constitutionalism and the Settlement of the West: The Attainment of Consensus, 1754–1784. In *The Territorial System*, ed. John Porter Bloom. Athens: Ohio University Press.

Bosniak, Linda. 2008. *The Citizen and the Alien: Dilemmas of Contemporary Membership*. Princeton: Princeton University Press.
Cabranes, Josê A. 1978. *Citizenship and Empire*. New Haven: Yale University Press.
Chen, B. 2014. Am. Sāmoa Army Recruiting Station Ranked #1 in the World. *Sāmoa News,* September 16.
Coletta, Paolo E. 1961. McKinley, the Peace Negotiations, and the Acquisition of the Philippines. *The Pacific Historical Review* 30 (4): 341.
Constitutional Accountability Center. *Citizenship, Immigration, and the Constitution*. http://www.theusconstitution.org/issue/citizenship. Accessed 8 June 2014.
de Tocqueville, Alexis. 2000. *Democracy in America*. New York: Bantam Classics.
Faleomavaega, Eni. 2012a. "An Unincorporated & Unorganized American Territory-Is This What American Sāmoa Wants?" Opinion Editorial. *Samoa News,* March 25.
Faleomavaega, Eni. 2012b. "Faleomavaega Introduces Legislation to Expedite Naturalization Process for U.S. Nationals." Press Release Statement, February 15. http://www.house.gov/list/press/as00_faleomavaega/expeditenaturalization forusnationalhtml.
Frederickson, George. 2002. *Racism, a Short Story*. Princeton: Princeton University Press.
Governor's Task Force Report on Population Growth. 2000. *Impacts of Rapid Population Growth in American Samoa: A Call to Action*. Report. Pago Pago: American Sāmoa.
Haney-Lopez, Ian. 2006. *White by Law: The Legal Construction of Race*. New York: New York University Press.
Kettner, James. 1978. *The Development of American Citizenship 1608–1870*. Chapel Hill: University of North Carolina Press.
Kettner, James. 2014. *The Development of American Citizenship, 1608–1870*. Chapel Hill, NC: The University of North Carolina Press.
Laughlin, Stanley K. 1984. The Burger Court and the United States Territories. *36 University of Florida Law Review* 755: 781–782.
Laughlin, Stanley K. 1995. *The Law of United States Territories and Affiliated Jurisdictions*. Eagan: Lawyers Cooperative Publishing.
Laughlin, Stanley K. 1996. The Application of the United States Constitution in the Territories: American Sāmoa, a Case Study. *2 University of Hawai'i Law Review* 44 (4): 675–678.
Langdell, Christopher C. 1899. The Status of Our New Territories. *Harvard Law Review* 6 (XII): 365–392.
Lee, Erica. 2007. *At America's Gates: Chinese Immigration During the Exclusionary Era, 1882–1943*. Chapel Hill: University of North Carolina Press.
Leech, Margaret. 1959. *In the Days of McKinley*. Newton: American Political Biography Press.

Lopez, Ian H. 1997. *White by Law: The Legal Construction of Race*. New York: New York Press.

May, Ernest R. 1968. *American Imperialism: A Speculative Essay*. Ann Arbor: University of Michigan.

Miller, Stuart Creighton. 1982. *Benevolent Assimilation: The American Conquest of the Philippines, 1899–1903*. New Haven: Yale University Press.

Ngai, Mae N. 2005. *Impossible Subjects: Illegal Aliens and the Making of Modern America*. Princeton: Princeton University Press.

O'Gorman, Benedict R. 2005. *Under Three Flags: Anarchism and the Anti-Colonial Imagination*. London: Verso.

Onuf, Peter S. 1987. *Statehood and Union: A History of the Northwest Ordinance*. Bloomington: Indiana University Press.

Pacific Island Reports. 1950. Hearings Before a Subcommittee on Interior & Insular Affairs, U.S.Sen., 81st Cong., 2nd Sess., on S.185, S.1892 and H.R. 7273: 61–65, April 19.

Park, C.B. 1972. *Population Studies of American Sāmoa: A Report to the Government of American Sāmoa*. Honolulu: East West Center.

Perea, Juan F. 2000. Fulfilling Manifest Destiny: Conquest, Race and the Insular Cases. In *Domestic in a Foreign Sense: Puerto Rico, American Expansion, and the Constitution*, ed. Christina Burnett and Burke Marshall. Durham: Duke University Press.

Pomeroy, Earl S. 1969. *The Territories and the United States, 1861–1890*. Seattle: University of Washington Press.

Ramos, Efrén R. 2001. Deconstructing Colonialism: 'The Unincorporated Territory' as a Category of Domination. In *Foreign in a Domestic Sense: Puerto Rico, American Expansion, and the Constitution*, ed. Christina Duffy Burnett and Burke Marshall. Durham: Duke University Press.

Randolph, Carman F., and Elmer Adams. 1898. Constitutional Aspects of Annexation. *Harvard Law Review* 5 (XII): 292–315.

Revised Constitution of American Sāmoa, art. 1, § 3.

Román, Ediberto. 1998. The Alien-Citizen Paradox and Other Consequences of Colonialism. *Florida State University Law Review* 26: 1.

Román, Ediberto. 2006. *The Other American Colonies: An International and Constitutional Law Examination of the United States' Nineteenth and Twentieth Century Island Conquests*. Durham: Carolina Academic Press.

Rossiter, Clinton, ed. 1961. *The Federalist Papers*. New York: Penguin Books.

S. Rep. No.94–1033 1976.

S. 1237 Omnibus Territories Act of 2013—113th Congress (2013–2014). https://beta.congress.gov/bill/113th-congress/senate-bill/1237/text.

Smith, Rogers M. 2001. The Bitter Roots of Puerto Rican Citizenship. In *Domestic in a Foreign Sense: Puerto Rico, American Expansion, and the Constitution*, ed. Christina D. Burnett and Burke Marshall. Durham: Duke University Press.

Ntumy, Michael A., Stephen A. Zorn, et al., eds. 1993. *South Pacific Legal Systems.* Honolulu: University of Hawai'i Press.

Sparrow, Bartholomew H. 2006. *The Insular Cases and the Emergency of American Empire.* Lawrence: University Press of Kansas.

Sunia, Fofo. 1988. *The Story of the Legislature of American Sāmoa: In Commemoration of the Golden Jubilee, 1948–1998.* Pago Pago: Legislature of American Sāmoa.

Thornbugh, Richard. 2001. Puerto Rican Separatism and United States Federalism. In *Foreign in a Domestic Sense: Puerto Rico, American Expansion, and the Constitution*, ed. Christina D. Burnett and Burke Marshall. Durham: Duke University Press.

Treaty of Paris, Dec. 10, 1898, art. IX, 39 Stat. 1754, 1759 (1899).

U.S. Department of Interior. Executive Order No. 10264, 3 C.F.R., 1949–1953 Comp. 765.

U.S. Department of Interior. Executive Order Number 10, 264, 16 Fed. Reg. 6419 (1951).

U.S. General Accountability Office. Nov. 1997. Report. *U.S. Insular Areas: Application of the U.S. Constitution.*

Van Dyke, Jon M. 1992. The Evolving Legal Relationships Between the United States and Its Affiliated U.S.-Flag Islands. *University of Hawaii Law Review* 14: 445–450.

Weinberg, Albert K. 1963. *Manifest Destiny: A Study of Nationalist Expansionism in American History.* Chicago: Quadrangle Books.

Welch, Richard E. 1972. *Imperialists Versus Anti-Imperialists: The Debate over Expansionism in the 1890s.* Itasca: F.E. Peacock Publishers.

Wells, Henry. 1971. The Modernization of Puerto Rico: A Political Study of Changing Values and Institutions. *Political Science Quarterly* 86 (1): 126–128.

Wise, John S. 1997. *A Treatise on American Citizenship.* Holmes Beach: Gaunt.

CHAPTER 6

American Sāmoan Legal History: 1900–1941

"It is not worthwhile for the Court to cite the numberless authorities on the question of the settlement of titles by adverse possession. The doctrine is so well understood that it is a waste of time to discuss it."
USN Commandant Charles Moore, Talala v. Logo,1 A.S.R. 166 at 174 (1907)

I do not want to hear any histories or stories that have been handed down—I want to know who has lived on these lands and has worked them for the past forty years—I will tell you why. I have never heard a story in this court that was handed down that the other side did not tell a story that was entirely different so that when we got thru [sic] I did not know which side to believe so it was just time wasted. The stories handed down in any family I do not know whether to believe them or not—what my father told me he saw I believe but anything else might very probably be made up in their mind.
USN Commandant Harry Wood, Saole v. Sagatu, 1-1919

The persistence of US-led negotiations with Great Britain and Germany throughout the mid-1800s over the Sāmoan Islands was not for riches, oil, or minerals, as was the case with South Africa and South America. The conquest of the Sāmoan Islands was important because it could aid expansionism and strengthen the American nationalistic spirit. The 1898 Spanish-American War catapulted the United States for the first time into international engagements, and the nation began to define itself as a country willing to engage in war to protect what it believed to be democratic

L.-N. Memea Kruse, *The Pacific Insular Case of American Sāmoa*,
https://doi.org/10.1007/978-3-319-69971-4_6

ideals. This war was a defining moment, one in which expansionism became entangled in the American narrative of upholding democracy after its own brutal Civil War. The "Splendid Little War" (as it was described by Theodore Roosevelt) fed the American political machine with victory and a belief that the Monroe Doctrine called for the United States to expand police democracy outside the Americas.

The 1899 Tripartite Treaty among Great Britain, Germany, and the United States carved up their Pacific Island interests among themselves without war. This was an achievement for the United States on the geopolitical front because of oceanic routes for commercial trade from Eastern Europe and East Asian countries. The main mission of the US military in the Sāmoan Islands was to secure a strong American presence, which it accomplished through the establishment of the Tutuila Naval Station. Germany had already established itself in the Independent State of Sāmoa with a bustling commercial and international trading post in Upolu.

USN Commandant Tilley was President of the High Court (the rough equivalent of a Chief Justice) and Edwin W. Gurr was one of the principal District Court Judges in the first decade of the Naval Administration. Gurr was by trade a lawyer, previously posted in the Independent State of Sāmoa working on land and title disputes. Eventually he became a member of the Commission investigating land disputes. The 1894 report of that Commission found that *papālagi* foreigners claimed more land acreage than the total area of Sāmoa (Amerika Samoa Humanities Council 2009, 49). Of the 1,250,270 acres of land claimed by Englishmen, only 36,000 acres, or about three percent, were confirmed; of the 134,419 acres of land claimed by German subjects, 75,000 acres, or about 56 percent, were confirmed; of the 302,746 acres claimed by American citizens, only 21,000 acres, or about seven percent, were confirmed; and of the 2307 acres claimed by the French, 1300 acres were confirmed (Ripine 2008, p. 345).

The USN Commandant was accountable only to the Secretary of the Navy, and without colonial administrative experience of island outposts, he was left to devise "democratic" governance mechanisms to create order and encourage obedience to the newly imposed American-styled rule of law. No other island territory or continental state had ever been accepted into the US body-politic through Deeds of Cession without a pathway to statehood being laid out. The USN Commandant created laws (administrative codes and regulations) without proper Naval guidance, a US Congressional mandate, or a Presidential roadmap for

American Sāmoa, and those laws were then replicated at the county level through village ordinances.

Between 1900 and 1902, the USN Commandant acted as the Commanding Officer for the US Naval fleet vis-à-vis the Department of Navy commission and handled the duties of the Governor without having received any formal commission. On April 2, 1902, two years after the arrival of the New Government—the American government administration—USN Commandant Sebree was named the first Governor over American Sāmoa by the Department of the Navy (Department of Navy 1902). Until 1902, the USN Commandant was commissioned to oversee the Tutuila Naval Station and assumed responsibility and authority as executive over American Sāmoa. Sebree responded with indifference to the Department of Navy's additional commission as Governor, writing to the US Assistant Secretary of Navy, "The Station, by Executive Order, comprises of all of the islands of the Samoan Group under our protection or sovereignty. I have, as Commandant, probably performed all the duties of Governor but I have no direct orders, appointment, or commission as Governor. I suppose it will make little or no difference in magnitude whether I am Governor or only Commandant, and personally I have no particular desires or wishes on the matter" (Sebree 1902).

What mattered most to the Department of State was the American position in the "American" Sāmoan Islands to be severed from the "German" Sāmoan Islands. Achieving a strong American position meant cutting the cultural ties between the two island groups. Renowned geographer John Coulter describes the cultural interconnectedness between the German Sāmoan Islands and American Sāmoan Islands in terms of the *mātai* title powers of Upolu over Tutuila:

> The land on Tutuila, once held by chiefs in the Atua District of East Upolu in Western Samoa [its former name under Germany], made Tutuila, as far as land tenure is concerned, an appendage of Upolu. Because subchiefs held the land in Tutuila in fief for their overlords in Upolu, when the government of Samoa was divided between Germany and the United States in 1900 the subchiefs on Tutuila were glad, for that meant they would probably be freed from their overlords in Upolu. Many titles of *mātai* on Tutuila [were] also originally from Atua District on Upolu. Because of the political separation of the two when the United States occupied the eastern islands, the chiefs on Tutuila have been able to attach more significance to their rank [than they could] when the islands were politically united. (Coulter 1957, pp. 80–95)

Customary Law and English Common Law Converge Over Communal Lands

In 1901, USN Commandant Tilley set out to monitor and regulate the alienation of customary lands to foreigners with procedures for registration, title searches in Lands Records, public notice of claims, and powers given to the Registrar to verify every land claim by foreigners (Regulation No. 2-1901). Other regulations followed during the US Navy's administration over the territory to restrict the alienation of "native lands" of indigenous Sāmoans to foreigners (Regulation 9-1906; Regulation No. 6, 1921). The powers and authority vested in *mātai* leadership over communal lands were (and are still currently) balanced between the state and local governance in the villages and districts.

The alienability of customary lands was, however, already a common practice of foreigners throughout the Sāmoan Islands. Most of the land alienated by foreigners was taken between 1860 and 1870 during the continual civil wars among Sāmoan clans and island groups. The influx of British, Germans, and Americans and their self-interested political alliances they made with clans, fueled by the importation of guns and ammunition, directly led *mātai* leaders to selling customary lands to purchase arms (Gilson 1970; Meleisea 1987). The Supreme Court of Sāmoa and the Commission found that ruling on land claim cases was not an easy process. The difficulty was deciding who had the actual powers to convey and transfer customary land; cases in dispute were caught between, on the one hand, the customary powers of the *fa'amātai* system, under which *pule* was held with the *mātai* and, on the other hand the legal bounds of "sale and disposition made by the rightful owner."[1]

Within the Sāmoan context, the "rightful owner" translates into *pule*, or right over the lands. Malietoa firmly addressed this issue in his correspondence with the Tripartite Treaty signatories; he insisted that "whoever sells land should have some lawful connection with the properties sold" (Malietoa 1894, p. 69). When the Commission attempted to define the legal parameters of *pule* within law, they decided that a chief:

> is simply guardian, without power of disposal, of tribal lands which, could not be sold. On the death of a Chief the tribal lands reverted to the community, and the control or 'pule' was conferred on his successor,[…] such successor not being necessarily the son of the former Chief […]. In some districts curious instances of associations of selected individuals, from Chiefs

> and others, were found acting as trustees, and so forming a regular trust, having the whole of the lands in the district under their control, but without power of disposal. (Haggard 1894, p. 14)

Essentially, the Court created land classifications that segmented customary lands. The classifications meant that land could be held by: (a) an individual, (b) a family (*āiga*), (c) a tribe [communities/villages] (*nu'u*), or (d) a district (*itūmālō*). The Court interpreted custom to create a legal status of "rightful owner" by extending the social and political parameters of *mātai pule* to include the legitimizing of rights over traditional lands. First, the Court developed the classification of "rightful owner." Second, the Court held that customary lands could be bought. Third, the Court held that consent of the *āiga* to customary lands controlled by the *mātai* was required to convey or transfer lands.

By the 1890s, the diminishing rights of the *mātai* over the conveyance or transfer of lands, coupled with the new system of different land classifications, led to the apportioning of customary lands. After foreigners had alienated large tracts of customary land in Independent State of Sāmoa in the 1860s and 1870s, alienation of customary land was introduced to American Sāmoa through adverse land possession. Adverse land possession in American Sāmoa was not about foreigners alienating customary land; Sāmoan families and individuals themselves sought to divide customary lands. The Navy was so preoccupied with trying to keep the resident Upolu *mātai* title holders from using their *mātai* titles to claim lands in American Sāmoa that no one considered the impacts that splitting customary lands through adverse possession would have upon the communal land holdings—not to mention their natural resources and access to those resources for future generations. Adverse land possession claims divided customary lands from family clan land holdings.

Traditionally, agricultural lands and village house sites are connected to specific *mātai* titles. These *mātai* titles and the customary lands connected to them are owned by the *āiga* and extended *āiga*, who operate under the leadership of the *mātai* title holders, who are selected by the *āiga*. The *mātai* and senior *mātai* decide what lands will be used for homes, agriculture, cooking spaces, *malae-fono* and *malae*, burial, cooking sites, open spaces, and what spaces will be reserved for future generations. Senior *mātai* also designate some communal land spaces for special purposes. There are three districts, and every district has a local "Governor" to oversee the counties under the district. The local government structure has remained intact throughout 115 years of the US Naval Administration, establishing a balance between Sāmoan custom and Western government. Under the district Governors, county councils, and village mayors ensure that all the villages within the counties are provided for and taken care of within the *fa'asāmoa* context; these officials are responsible for mediating disputes, addressing village concerns and distributing resources among each other. The county councils and village mayors, along with the senior *mātai* of each village, distribute parcels of land to each *āiga* clan to build houses and formal meeting spaces and structures for senior *mātai* and lesser *mātai*, and they allocate lands to be used for agriculture, for access ways for villages to natural resources during times of need (daily and *fa'alavelave*), and for access roads and new schools. Any time a person or *āiga* desires to build a structure or piggery, or to conduct business activity on communal lands, consent and approval by the *Sa'o* is required. *Fa'asāmoa* lives and breathes because the foundation is service, sharing, distribution, redistribution, dialogue, consensus, decision-making, and punishment that happens within each village, county, and district on communal lands. The *fa'asāmoa* has survived American governance for over 115 years because the *fa'amātai*, the distribution and use of communal lands by Sāmoans within villages, continues to be practiced and protected by local Constitution. However, the population growth and demographics of American Sāmoa have changed greatly, and the dividing of customary lands through adverse possession is threatening its very survival.

Adverse Land Possession: Ten Years of Continuous Cultivation and Possession

Between the 1840s and 1870s, alienation of Sāmoan customary lands flourished, which prompted social and cultural unrest that led the Commission to investigate many land claims. It wasn't just *papālagi* claims to land; the political jockeying between foreigners, Sāmoan civil wars, and violent hostilities also led to new political alliances, reshaping of districts to strengthen clans with foreign supporters, and claims to larger tracts of land.[2] Missionaries, sailors, beachcombers, and *papālagi* land speculators maximized the numerous civil wars to further their interests in the appropriation of customary land between the 1840s and 1860s in Apia (downtown) and the Ā'ana district. Thomas Trood, who served as British Vice Consul in Sāmoa during the 1900s when Germany annexed Sāmoa, described alienation of land:

> Having taken possession of Apia and all the coast line in the north side of Upolu, the victors began to sell the land of their enemies, and as they were in want of money, disposed of it at very cheap rates. In consequence of this the latter when they returned to Apia many months later were disagreeably surprised at the course of events had taken, and many disputes arose between them and the foreigners who had acquired their land, some of which were carried to the courts, but I am unable to say with what results, excepting that in one or two cases which came under my notice, such war titles were declared valid; that fact not protecting the occupants against the repeated attempts of the original owners to regain possession. Certainly such sales ought to have been barred by authorities. (Trood 1917, p. 85)

By 1889, the Commission found that *papālagi* land claims were more than double the entire land area of Sāmoa. Therefore, the Commission needed to establish firm legal principles governing what constituted legal title and claim to land (Chambers 1895, p. 459). The Commission resorted to the 1899 Berlin Treaty Article IV, section 10 to prevent the alienation of customary lands (Keesing 1934, p. 258). The section states that "Sāmoans should keep their lands for cultivation by themselves and by their children after them;" however, it also validated title to land through adverse land possession principles to allow aliens legitimate and lawful rights to title of lands. It reads:

> undisputed possession and continuous cultivation of lands by aliens for **ten years or more [should] constitute a valid title** by prescription to the lands so cultivated: land acquired in good faith and subsequently improved upon the basis of a title found defective might be confirmed in whole or in part upon payment, by the occupant to the person or persons entitled thereto, of an additional sum to be ascertained by the Commission and approved by the Court as equitable and just (emphasis added). (Gilson 1970, p. 407)

Legal doctrine thus established that continuous cultivation for ten years and undisputed possession legitimized land claims in the Court. For the first time in the history of the Sāmoan archipelago, adverse possession rights were established to validate claims on customary lands vis-à-vis the 1899 Treaty of Berlin. The US Supreme Court relied on these adverse possession principles to advance legitimate title to land that met the conditions of "undisputed possession and continuous cultivation of lands by aliens for tens or more," conditions that were taken directly from English common law which stated that "a possession of another's land which, when accompanied by certain acts and circumstances, will vest title in the possessor" (2 Corpus Juris 50).[3] Successful claimants in the US Supreme Court returned back to American Sāmoa to enforce the Court's decisions.

Incorporating Civility and Stabilization to Land Titles, Naval High Court

In the first 40 years of the Naval High Court, the statutory period for recovery of land by adverse land possession increased from 10 to 20 to 30 years of undisputed possession and cultivation. Adverse land possession became a sword to divide communal lands from the family's land holding under the *fa'asāmoa* structure of the *mātai* title system. Splitting of communal lands by evidence of possession and cultivation was done without care to the *fa'asāmoa*, communal land tenure, displacement of family clans held together by communal lands under the stewardship of the *fa'amātai*.

The USN Commandants were military men, dispatched to the US Naval Station in Tutuila to advance the mandates of nation-building, and very little, if any, attention was given to how the laws they established negatively affect the traditional land tenure and, therefore, local traditions and customs. Indigenous culture was not a consideration within the legal framework of the initial American administration in American Sāmoa (*Talala v. Logo*, 1 A.S.R. 166, 171 (1907)). In 1907, the High Court, which was composed of Naval personnel who were not necessarily trained in law, stated that "within ages not so very remote [...] titles often changed hands by force more or less violent, and that one of the recognized modes of transfer was war, or force." The Naval judges believed it was their responsibility to stabilize land titles under the new American administration. One ruling declared:

> In this world of uncertainty the gradual progress of civilization tends to eliminate uncertainties, and one of the blessings of civilization is the stability of land titles. A competent court setting forth that after a proper trial he was awarded title to the land, will not be disturbed in his possession after a lapse of many years, unless extraordinary circumstances are shown justifying exceptional action by another Court. (*Tialavea v. Aga*, 3 A.S.R. 272, 275 (1957))

USN Commandant Charles Moore, also President of the High Court and Governor of American Sāmoa, unequivocally supported adverse land possession rights because these rights were accepted by "civilized" countries.[4] USN Commandant-Governor Moore declared, "It is not worthwhile for this Court to cite the numberless authorities on the question of the settlement of titles by adverse possession. The doctrine is so well understood that it is a waste of time to discuss it" (*Talala v. Logo*, 1 A.S.R. 166, 177 at 174 (1907)). Judge Arthur A. Morrow, in justifying the usage of adverse land possession principles, states that the American court of law is based upon English common law:

> It requires no argument to reach the conclusion that the Statute of 21 James I, Chap. 16, passed by the English parliament in 1623 and, with certain exceptions, limiting actions for the recovery of property to a period within twenty years after the accrual of the right of action, is applicable and suitable to conditions in American Samoa in the absence of a provision in the Codification prescribing a period within which actions to recover real property may be brought after the accrual right to sue. Nor are the provisions of that statute 'repugnant to or inconsistent with the Constitution and laws of the United States of America.' We think that the phrase English common law as used in Sec. 3(1) should be interpreted to include such acts of the English parliament as were in force at the time of the American Revolution and are suitable to conditions in American Samoa. It is our opinion that the Statute of 21 James I, Chap. 16, is a part of the law of American Samoa. (*Talo v. Poi*, 2 A.S.R. 66 (1938))[5]

The first USN Commandant of the American Sāmoa naval station and acting Governor, Benjamin Tilley, further justified these local laws by proclaiming, "The Court has found it imperative—absolutely necessary—to follow the practice that is general practice now in every civilized portion of the earth and that is to recognize that the occupancy of the land for a fixed period constitutes ownership of the land" (*Leiato v. Howden*, 1 A.S.R. 45 (1901)).[6] Tilley also presided over a case of Manu'a lands (prior to the Deed of Cession over the Manu'a Islands) in 1900, during the fledgling years of the American Government administration. In *Lagoo v. Mao*, Tilley applies possession, cultivation, and the ten-year standard for awarding land rights in Ofu to establish clear claim of right to title of the land (*Lagoo v. Mao*, 1 A.S.R. 15 (1900)).

USN Commandant-Governor Uriel Sebree affirmed the rights of adverse land possession in *Laapui v. Taua* by stating that "besides proving his cause as alleged in the particulars of the claim hereon, [the claimant has] been in undisputed possession and cultivation of the land in dispute for a period exceeding a term of 10 years prior to the dispute which occurred, forming the cause of the action, and such occupation gives a prescriptive title of the land" (*Laapui v. Taua,* 1 A.S.R. 24 (1901)).[7] USN Commandant-Governor Edmund Underwood in 1903 decided in favor of the party that had demonstrated "continuous cultivation and undisputed possession for a period of over ten (10) years" and therefore had "acquired legal title to all cultivated portion of land" (*Fatialofa v. Fagamalo*, LT. No. 5-1903).[8] In 1903, Chaplain of the Naval Station and President of the High Court B.R. Patrick stated that the ten-year period of possession was the law over land title disputes in the "colony" (*Tufaga v. Liufau,* 1 A.S.R. 184 (1903)).[9] Additionally, in the *Tuatoo v. Faumuina* case Patrick determined that the rights to title of Alofao lands were evidenced by continuous use and occupation by the plaintiffs. In 1907, Patrick divided parcels of Faletele lands between claimants using adverse land principles of possession and cultivation to decide between directly contradictory testimonies.

USN Commandant Samuel Henderson in *Tupuola v. Togia* decided to award the lands Maia, Lotopa, Afaga, and Leoneuli to the plaintiff and Lotopa land to the defendant based on the strongest testimony of continuous possession. Chief Justice Harry Wood, exasperated with the conflicting and confusing testimony given in the Court, pronounced, "all we care about is who has used this land openly and notoriously with a claim of right to the land and everyone knows he has used the land and has planted *taro* and banana on it for the past thirty years, that is all we want to know" (*Saole v. Sagatu,* LT. No. 1-1919).[10] In 1931, Wood felt propelled to pen an article in the *Le Faatonu* (Government Gazette) about the nature and purpose of the Courts because he still felt the Sāmoan people didn't understand the Court system and needed instruction and guidance on how to legitimately bring forward land and *mātai* title disputes in the Courts (Wood 1936, pp. 3–4). In *Saole v. Sagatu,* Wood also stated that in America there are deeds to show clear ownership of land, while in American Sāmoa all there is to prove ownership is who is using the land for a long time, "planting bananas, taro, [and] coconuts" (*Saole v. Sagatu,* LT. No. 1-1919).[11]

For the first 30 to 40 years, military Commandants over the High Court enforced adverse possession because they considered it part of civilized society to recognize and practice the recovery of lands through a select set of elements. There was a high turnover rate of USN military commandants in the Tutuila Naval Station; within each decade at least three to four different commandants presided over the High Court, not including the substitute naval personnel like USN Chaplain Patrick who had assumed leadership of the High Court during their leave periods. Each naval officer that became commandant and president of the High Court believed in the ability of an individual to adversely claim land against another, because they believed it reflected a civilized procedure for mediating land claims and that its legal foundation was grounded in civilized society. This introduction of the concept of "civilization" as a legal standard in American Sāmoa was also a form of "Americanization" because it entailed the idea that the individual man has universal rights superseding any indigenous cultural customs. While the administration prevented alienation of customary lands from foreigners, there was no protection to safeguard tracts of customary (communal) lands from individuals within Sāmoan villages.

Moneyed Economy, Cultivation, Taxes

USN Commandant Tilley negotiated with the *mātai* during the Deeds of Cession talks was later commissioned to be the first commandant at the Naval Station. USN Commandant Tilley employed an "indirect rule" governance system over the territory without any guidance or direction from the Navy brass. Between 1900 and 1905, before the title of Governor was officially added to the commandant's commission, this "indirect rule" was employed by all the USN commandants. Tilley created an administrative structure and established three districts—Eastern, Western, and Manu'a—to oversee purely local matters, with a Samoan *mātai* over each district. Each of the three districts was divided into 14 counties, each with a county chief. The counties were classified into 52 villages. Every village had a *pulenu'u*, village council, and a council of *mātai*. *Pulenu'u* are liaisons between the customary Sāmoan system of government and central government. The traditional Sāmoan systems of government are the *mātai*, high *mātai*, talking *mātai*, and village council.

Since the High Court was the administrative arm of the civil administration, the military instituted policy through the enactment of laws. There were no judiciary or legislative branches. The USN Commandant appointed local government heads, Secretary of Native Affairs, judges, and secretarial staff in naval offices. Tilley single-handedly created the 1900 Promulgation and Publication of Law, expressly recognizing and allowing the adverse possession of land by declaring that "No motion for the recovery of real property or for the recovery of the possession thereof, can be maintained unless it appear that the plaintiff, his ancestor or predecessor was united or possessed of the property in question within ten years before the commencement of the motion" (US Promulgation and Publication of Law 1900, No. 1). Without branches of government to check and balance the executive authority of the USN Commandant, the governance system in place could be viewed as an autocracy. The USN Commandant had complete power over the territory while the US federal branches of government ignored the military entanglements in the American Sāmoan territory. The USN Commandant could and did create, interpret, and enforce law and order.

The USN Commandants levied copra taxes against each village to sustain government operations (US Navy Regulation Numbers 21-1900, 1-1917, 3-1921). Cultivation and taxes were necessary to start a money economy in American Sāmoa, a change necessary to conduct business as a US territory. Cultivation is a principal element of adverse land possession; a claimant must show evidence that they farmed the land, a feat that became easier to prove when the military regulated the cultivation of lands for copra taxes. Copra taxes were paid by Sāmoans in each district through copra, the sale of which would go directly to the US military for the operations of government.[12] Therefore, each village was mandated by military proclamations that every *mātai*, family, and person cultivate their lands to produce enough agricultural staples to pay the government the monthly copra tax. Table 6.1 outlines the village ordinances mandating cultivation for taxation purposes and the imposition of fines when not obeyed.

The USN Commandant also issued concurrent ordinances mandating that each village live a clean, orderly, and respectable lifestyle. Village ordinances reflected the newly imposed Christian-American values. Village punishment and fines were also collected against certain indigenous practices substituted with western values. A moneyed economy was enforced through payment for food replacing resource distribution in the village under the control of the *mātai*, nationalism was enforced through flag raising and salute, traditional tattooing was outlawed, *malagas* were forbidden, and communal sharing was prohibited among the family clans. In the village of Afono, no person could bathe naked in the village pools, and illicit cohabitation was forbidden. Each family was required to have a banana and taro plantation, and all families were required to have curtains in the windows and care for the curtains (Village of Afono 1900, Village Laws). In the village of Alao, fornication was prohibited, and every family was required to plant coconuts, bananas, and sugar cane (Village of Alao 1900, Village Laws).

Table 6.1 Village cultivation ordinances, 1900s

Village	*Cultivation ordinance*	*Civility ordinance*	*Fine*
Afao		Illicit cohabitation prohibited Scandal is prohibited	If no fine specified, Court to determine punishment not to exceed $10.00
Afono	***Mātai*** must have a sugar cane plantation Each family must have giant *taro*, banana, plantation	Illicit cohabitation prohibited No nakedness or nuisance in public bathing place Each family must take care of curtains No person allowed to defecate in the bush	If no fine specified, Court to determine punishment not to exceed $10.00
Aitulagi	Each person must have a *taro* plantation Every person must plant five coconuts, five bananas, and five ta´amū[a] plants monthly ***Mātai*** must have sugar cane plantation	No defecation in village No one can give away for free *taro*, banana, coconut—there must be payment for all food Illicit cohabitation prohibited	If no fine specified, Court to determine punishment not to exceed $10.00
Alao	Plant coconuts, sugar cane, and bananas	Fornication prohibited Roads, houses, drinking water, bathing places shall be kept in good order	Fine for not planting—weed public road for 50 fathoms
Alofau	Sugar cane was taboo to eat or give away (it could only be bought from the chief for $5.00) Everyone must cultivate	Illicit cohabitation prohibited Prohibited to spread gossip or slander another	Punishment will be given for not cultivating, the specific punishment is not listed
Amaluia	Everyone must cultivate Prohibited to cut sugar cane (except for copra taxes)	Forbidden for men to court women in the ***'aualuma***[b]	Fine for not cultivating—$0.50

(*continued*)

Table 6.1 (continued)

Village	*Cultivation ordinance*	*Civility ordinance*	*Fine*
Onenoa	Everyone must plant *ta'amū* and banana plantation All lands since the New Government be in good order	Illicit cohabitation prohibited Nuisance in bathing places prohibited	If no fine specified, Court to determine punishment not to exceed $10.00
Pago Pago	Every person must plant 50 bananas, 50 coconuts, 20 ta´amū, 25 taro every year Every ***mātai*** must have a sugar cane plantation	Fornication is prohibited Village and public roads must be cleaned every month Everyone must bath with a lava lava Gambling prohibited Everyone must salute the US flag	Fornication fine not to exceed $5.00 Fine—$2.00 for anyone not planting
Poloa	Every person must have a taro plantation	Illicit cohabitation prohibited	If no fine specified, Court to determine punishment not to exceed $10.00
Seetaga	Every person must plant 5 coconuts, 15 bananas, 5 kava roots, 5 ta´amū plants	All sinnet must be sold	If no fine specified, Court to determine punishment not to exceed $10.00
Taputimu	Every family must cultivate sugar cane plantation Every man must plant taro, coconut plantation		Fine for not cultivating—$0.50
Tula	Sugar cane and bananas must be planted	Illicit cohabitation prohibited	Cohabitation fine—weed the public road 100 fathoms

[a] *Ta'amū* is a variety of giant *taro*

[b]' *Aualuma* is the unmarried women's group in the village

[c] *Malaga* was considered a high expense by the USN

> Court and then you always know that the other man is living on the land thru [sic] your permission; but they do not do that in Samoa—they let it go for generations and generations. There are many cases where the man in the United States where a man lets the people walk across his land and every year or so he puts a rope up to keep the people off and if he lets them do it for 20 years without putting up a rope he can never stop them. (*Avegalio v. Suafoa,* 1 A.S.R. 476 (1932))

Early in their administration, USN commandants tried to protect communal lands from foreigners, largely because Gurr had seen firsthand the scale of the land grabbing by gluttonous foreign speculators. However, the commandants did not foresee the internal splitting of communal lands and the possible negative effects on the land tenure system in the future. Internal splitting of communal lands was also performed by Sāmoans and *mātai* title holders, from Upolu who claimed rights to lands in American Sāmoa. Due to the ongoing civil wars throughout the Sāmoan archipelago in the 1800s, many *mātai* title holders would move between *āiga* lands in the Independent State of Sāmoa and those in American Sāmoa, seeking the one that would best position them with power, authority, and leadership in the village. If a *mātai* was given a senior *mātai* title in a village from Independent State of Sāmoa, he would move there and change his name to the *mātai* title appointed to him.[17] *Mātai* title holders in the Independent State of Sāmoa would relocate to American Sāmoa if the *mātai* title was of higher significance and afforded more prestige, power, and authority. The USN commandants considered the *mātai* title holders from Upolu a threat to the American territory because they were not domiciled there. *Mātai* title holders from the Independent State of Sāmoa represented non-Americans trying to assert their rights on American soil through land ownership and *mātai* influence. Because of the military's aspiration to advance American presence and political power in the region, in the first decade of the court system the Naval High Court emphasized separation of Independent Sāmoa from American Sāmoa. The military feared that, if the higher-ranking chiefs in Upolu all claimed adverse title to lands, no lands would be left to Native American Sāmoans. During the first half of the twentieth century, USN Commandant Tilley was the strongest proponent of protecting the lands from Upolu *mātai*. In the first two years of the High Court, he made it very clear that occupancy and cultivation was required for ten years of all adverse claimants and that Upolu chiefs must prove this positively for any adverse landsuits.

Land and Changing Society

Following the signing of the Tripartite Treaty in 1899, the American government demonstrated that they were a much better protector against foreigners alienating customary lands than Upolu's protectorate—Germany. US military convoys noticed that in Independent State of Sāmoa there were huge tracts of prime land claimed (many fraudulently) by foreigners, which led the early US administration in Tutuila to enact legislation to prevent that. These actions, although seemingly altruistic, were in fact a display of the US government's protectionism over its territorial outpost, part of its political maneuvering to become a power player in the Asia-Pacific region.

Modern writings about American Sāmoa's customary lands refer mostly to the Deeds of Cession and its protections of customary lands which the United States is bound to protect. However, the influences of the nineteenth century Berlin and Tripartite Treaties established a different conceptual legal framework, forming the norms and molding the customs used to construct an Americanized lifestyle. US recognition and acceptance of land court decisions from Sāmoa's Supreme Court and its Land Commission is not surprising; the Courts defined a rightful owner of customary lands based upon English common law, which is the basis of American common law. Sāmoa's Courts apportioned customary lands. Land classifications distinguished lands that could be owned by an individual, family, tribe, or district. These land classifications fueled the legitimacy of established land rights within each class of society. The USN commandants embraced these land classifications and decisions from sovereign Sāmoa. The USN commandants were not legally trained and their first and foremost priority was the commission of commandant at the Tutuila Naval Station; the added responsibility of Commandant-Governor assignment, judicial functions, and taxation were secondary priorities. The importation of legal decisions from Sāmoa's bench based on imported common law principles and decisions rendered by *papālagis* assigned through the plenipotentiary signatories of the Berlin Treaty made it that much easier to validate the western legal concepts of the individual and adverse land possession. Deutsch-Sāmoa's Supreme Court applied the land classifications in the Berlin Treaty. American Sāmoa's early Commandant-Governors gladly accepted their land verdicts to establish civil order under the Berlin Treaty organizing principles.

USN Commandant-Governors were hard-pressed to stabilize land title claims without written deeds or surveys. On the one hand, they were motivated to provide evidence that American Sāmoa was progressing toward "civilization" and the American way of life under their watch. The moneyed economy and capitalistic spirit led to regulations to force cultivation; every sinnet (coconut husk), *taro*, breadfruit, and banana required monetary payment, and nothing could be given away for free. Customary acts of exchanging food among neighbors, families, visitors, and villages were prohibited. On the other hand, while the USN commandants were united in their opposition to alienation of lands to foreigners, there was a growing desire by Sāmoans to own lands separate from the village, which the principles of adverse land possession readily accommodated. USN commandants favored *mātais* from Tutuila over Upolu, because doing so protected American interests domestically and, given the restrictive nature of evidentiary testimony to stabilize land claims, created a pathway for individuals to recover lands based solely on cultivation and possession, rather than on the village and *mātai* structure. Adverse possession apportioned customary lands. The guiding principles to claim lands were not based on hereditary right to title or *āiga* affiliation but rather upon who had the strongest evidence of continuous occupation and undisputed possession to prove their claim.

Sāmoans could have negated all these naval decisions had they chosen to appear before the Judicial Commission. The Judicial Commission was comprised of high ranking *mātai* (no foreigners) selected by county "Governors" to hear land and *mātai* disputes. USN commandants advocated that all land and *mātai* cases first seek their cases to be calendared among their peers by the Judicial Commission, because they were then eligible for appeal to the High Court. Cases that were heard in the High Court were not eligible for appeal. USN Commandants Wood and Johnson pleaded with litigants to present cases before the Judicial Commission, and Sāmoan district judge Muli reminded the litigants that it was to their advantage to present their cases to their Sāmoan peers (*Saole v. Safatu*, 1-1919; *Satele v. Afoa,* 1 A.S.R. 467 (1932)).[18] However, no case was ever tried before the Judicial Commission and the pleas by the High Court fell on deaf ears. This could be for two reasons: first, because Sāmoan litigants preferred their cases tried not by their peers whom they believed to be biased about land disputes but instead before the Naval High Court; or second, the litigants may have wanted to have their case tried in the highest court possible due to the importance of customary land to Sāmoans.

Americanization doesn't happen in a vacuum; elements of western lifestyle were mandated by village ordinances that made certain customs illegal. The earliest ordinances punished individuals for "illicit cohabitation," thereby requiring adherence to western practices of matrimony and domesticity in the village. Nakedness, public displays of the body, traditional tattooing, cricket games, and *malagas* between villages and islands were all prohibited, to be replaced with American traditions and practices. It was not hard to see that a shift to "individual" land ownership was on the horizon. The legal pathway to owning land individually, apart from the family and village, was foreseeable. The further dividing of customary lands was just a matter of time, as the desires of an "I" lifestyle are part and parcel of being American.

Notes

1. At that time, the only Court system was using Art. IV, Sec. 8 of the Final Act of Berlin as a prescriptive section, confirming claims concluded prior to the Tripartite Treaty. See Section 10: "the equitability of consideration received in exchange for land"; Section 4, "whether the land was sold by those empowered to do so, 'by the rightful owner' [...] for sufficient consideration;" Section 11, "with clear or regular title identifying boundaries."
2. Warfare was forever changed by the European sailors bartering with and selling of ammunition and guns. The introduction of guns and weapons changed the nature of warfare between clans and districts, making their conflicts much more violent and leading to higher rates of death and mutilation.
3. "The possession must be actual, visible, exclusive, hostile, and continued during the time necessary to create a bar under the statute of limitations."
4. Charles Moore was USN Commandant and Governor from January 1905 to May 1908.
5. Arthur Morrow was chief justice from 1937 to 1966.
6. Benjamin Tilley was the first USN Commandant and acting Governor from 1899 to 1901 (left American Sāmoa after being court martialed).
7. Uriel Sebree was USN Commandant and Governor from January 1905 to May 1908.
8. Edmund Underwood was USN Commandant and Governor from May 1903 to January 1905.
9. B.R. Patrick was the Chaplain of the Naval Station and was assigned the President of the High Court during periods when the USN Commandant left the islands on holiday.
10. Harry Wood was chief justice from 1921 to 1937.

11. The limitation of 20 years to claim title through adverse land possession was also applied by the High Court to prohibit land claims due to the statute of limitation. In *Tuiolosega v. Voa*, 2 ASR 138 (1941), the High Court denied the plaintiff's adverse land claim over land in Olosega because the plaintiff filed against *Voa* in 1918 but only prosecuted his claim to recover possession in 1941, meaning that the plaintiff did not exercise due diligence. The High Court determined that because Tuiolosega waited for 23 years to prosecute his case, his suit did not stop the clock to the running of the statute.
12. Each district had a certain amount of pounds required to be brought to government for sale. Bigger districts were required to provide more than smaller districts in terms of poundage of copra.
13. "In view of the fact that so much time has been wasted in the beginning of this year in cricket games between villages, no permission will be granted for *malagas* until further orders. No *malaga* will be made at any time for any purpose without the approval of the Governor." Cricket games became so widely played that food production was seriously affected, and the civil government and religious missions became so concerned that they made cricket playing a disciplinary offense, not just in Sāmoa but also in Tonga, K. Fortune (2000), "Cricket," p.459. Henry Bryan was USN Commandant and Governor from March 1925 to September 1927.
14. In the first 15 years of the American administration, there was really just one surveyor on the islands that completed surveys as required by the High Court, American merchant B.F. Kneubuhl.
15. While the High Court considered the names of the communal lands irrelevant, the village names are important to the village. The names may represent Sāmoan legends, war, significant natural resource on the lands, or symbolism of something unique and tangible to the village.
16. *Poumuli* is the Sāmoan and Tongan name for a tree that is very durable and used as poles for traditional homes and cooking houses, also known as *Securinega flexuosa*.
17. Sāmoan names do not conform to western practices of name-giving from birth to death. In the Sāmoan custom, the child may take the father's surname and/or the *mātai* as the first name. Then, upon conveyance of *mātai* title later in life, the individual then assumes the *mātai* title as the first name and the father's name as the last name. In addition, the individual may possess a *mātai* title, then receive a more senior *mātai* title from the village *mātai*, at which point the individual will change their name again to reflect the senior *mātai* title as the first name. The most senior and prestigious *matai* name will be ordered as the first name.
18. In order to have a case tried before the Judicial Commission, both parties to the lawsuit must agree to have their dispute heard by the Judicial Commission. If one party refused to have the case heard by the Judicial Commission, then the case was heard before the High Court.

References

Avegalio v. Suafoa, 1 A.S.R. 476 (1932).
Fatialofa v. Fagamalo, LT. No. 5-1903.
Laapui v. Taua, 1 A.S.R. 24 (1901).
Lagoo v. Mao, 1 A.S.R. 15 (1900).
Lauvao v. Misipaga, 1 A.S.R. 105 (1907).
Leiato v. Howden, 1 A.S.R. 45 (1901).
Saole v. Sagatu, 1-1919.
Satele v. Afoa, 1 A.S.R. 467 (1932).
Talala v. Logo,1 A.S.R. 166 at 174 (1907).
Talo v. Poi, 2 A.S.R. 9 (1938).
Tialavea v. Aga, 3 A.S.R. 272, 275 (1957).
Tufaga v. Liufau, 1 A.S.R. 184 (1903).
Tupuola v. Togia,1 A.S.R. 270 (1912).
Tupuola v. Togia. 1903. A Regulation Relating to Samoan Traveling Parties Between the Islands of Savaii and Upolu and the Islands of Tutuila and Manua. No. 2, March 30.
Amerika Sāmoa Humanities Council. 2009. *A History of American Sāmoa*. Korea.
Bryan, Henry F. 1927. Order Issued, March 8.
Chambers, William L. 1895. *Report of W.L. Chambers United States Land Commissioner to Samoa*. United States Congress 53-3, Senate Ex. Doc No. 97, Message from the President … Transmitting Correspondence Touching Samoan Affairs. Washington, DC.
Coulter, John W. 1957. *The Pacific Dependencies of the United States*. New York: Macmillan Company.
Crocombe, Ron. 1987. *Land Tenure in the Pacific*. 3rd ed. Suva: University of South Pacific.
Fortunte, Kate. 2000. Cricket. In *The Pacific Islands: An Encyclopedia*, ed. Brij Lal and Kate Fortune. Honolulu: University of Hawai'i Press.
Gilson, Richard P. 1970. *Sāmoa 1830 to 1900: The Politics of a Multi-Cultural Community*. London: Oxford University Press.
Haggard, Bazett M. 1894. *Report by Way of Memorandum of the Working and Transactions of the Samoan Land Commission between May 24, 1891, and December 31, 1894*. Great Britain, Foreign Office, Pacific Islands, Navigators, Confidential Prints, 14, July–December.
Keesing, Felix. 1934. *Modern Sāmoa: Its Government and Changing Life*. London: George Allen & Unwin.
Malietoa Letter to British Foreign Office. 1894. Confidential Prints Correspondence January–June 1894, FO 534/65, 69, March 28.
Meleisea, Malama. 1987. *The Making of Modern Samoa: Traditional Authority and Colonial Administration in the Modern History of Western Samoa*. Suva: Institute of the South Pacific.

Ripine, Muli'aumaseali'i A. 2008. *A History of Amerika Samoa: An Annotated Timeline*. Pago Pago: American Samoa Community College.
Sebree, Uriel. 1902. Uriel Sebree Letter to U.S. Assistant Secretary of the Navy, April 7.
Tilley, Benjamin F. 1990. Promulgation and Publication of Law No. 1.
Tilley, Benjamin F. 1900. Promulgation and Publication of Law No. 21-1900.
Tilley, Benjamin F. 1901. Promulgation and Regulation No. 2-1901. Provisional Regulation Regarding Titles to Land.
Trood, Thomas. 1917. *Island Reminiscences*. Bibliolife: online.
U.S. Promulgation and Publication of Law, 1-1917.
U.S. Promulgation and Publication of Law, 3-1912.
Village of Afono. 1900. Village Laws. American Sāmoa Government Research and Archive Microfiche Reel 9, Series 12; Reel 10, Series 12.
Village of Aoa. 1900. Village Laws. American Sāmoa Government Research and Archive Microfiche Reel 9, Series 12; Reel 10, Series 12.
Village of Alao. 1900. Village Laws. American Sāmoa Government Research and Archive Microfiche Reel 9, Series 12; Reel 10, Series 12.
Village of Alofau. 1900. Village Laws. American Sāmoa Government Research and Archive Microfiche Reel 9, Series 12; Reel 10, Series 12.
Village of Amouli. 1900. Village Laws. American Sāmoa Government Research and Archive Microfiche Reel 9, Series 12; Reel 10, Series 12.
Village of Fagaitua. 1900. Village Laws. American Sāmoa Government Research and Archive Microfiche Reel 9, Series 12; Reel 10, Series 12.
Village of Faganeanea and Matu'u. 1900. Village Laws. American Sāmoa Government Research and Archive Microfiche Reel 9, Series 12; Reel 10, Series 12.
Village of Fagasa. 1900. Village Laws. American Sāmoa Government Research and Archive Microfiche Reel 9, Series 12; Reel 10, Series 12.
Village of Fagatogo. 1900. Village Laws. American Sāmoa Government Research and Archive Microfiche Reel 9, Series 12; Reel 10, Series 12.
Village of Lauli'i. 1900. Village Laws. American Sāmoa Government Research and Archive Microfiche Reel 9, Series 12; Reel 10, Series 12.
Village of Nu'uuli. 1900. Village Laws. American Sāmoa Government Research and Archive Microfiche Reel 9, Series 12; Reel 10, Series 12.
Village of Onenoa. 1900. Village Laws. American Sāmoa Government Research and Archive Microfiche Reel 9, Series 12; Reel 10, Series 12.
Village of Pago Pago. 1900. Village Laws. American Sāmoa Government Research and Archive Microfiche Reel 9, Series 12; Reel 10, Series 12.
Wood, Harry. 1936. "Your Courts, Their Nature and Purpose." *Le Faatonu*, January, 3–4.

CHAPTER 7

Individually Owned Lands and Communal Land Tenure

"When a village was established, the land in that village belonged to the people of that village. A mātai could claim land for his family or clan by clearing and then working it. Any land that was not under the direct 'pule' of a mātai remained belonging to the people of the village. Paramount chiefs would have a more general control of larger areas. It is important to keep in mind that the power of a mātai was really defined not by title name, but by the land which he had control. Through this system, ownership of land from the mountain peak to the reef was defined among the various families, villages, and districts."
Leuma v. Willis, LT 047-79, slip op. at 4 (Land and Titles Div. Dec. 16, 1980)

Early land cases under the Naval Administration established the legal pathway to alienate land by the court-established classification of individually owned land. Indigenous Sāmoans, wanting to own land for themselves apart from the *āiga* and village, have been participants in the splitting of communal lands.

The unabated and unmonitored growth of registered individually owned lands materializes the fear of the 1979 Territorial Planning Commission. They cautioned that Sāmoans would convert communally owned lands into individually owned lands because there was a growing "minority of Sāmoans that wanted to break free from communal obligations," in part so that these lands could be then willed to their children.

L.-N. Memea Kruse, *The Pacific Insular Case of American Sāmoa*,
https://doi.org/10.1007/978-3-319-69971-4_7

They foresaw that Americanization would begin to take hold in the territory and that Sāmoans would want to own land separate from the obligations of the *fa'amātai* structure. In the 1979 case *Craddick v. Territorial Registrar of American Samoa*, the petitioners asserted that individually owned lands comprised less than four percent of all lands in American Sāmoa (*Craddick v. Territorial Registrar of American Samoa*, CA 61-78, slip op. (Trial Div. May 10, 1979) (Order Denying Motion for New Trial or Rehearing Civil Action No. 61-78)). There has been a significant increase in individually owned lands from 1979, when less than four percent of lands were individually owned to 2013, when 25.7 percent are now registered as individually owned (Statistical Yearbook 2013, p. 97).

Decisions and Vernacular Language Usage in High Court, Tracing Individual Ownership

In land dispute cases from 1900 involving adverse land possession and individually owned land dispute decisions, foreign rights to native lands were based upon the Court's determination that the best evidence of land ownership is through dominion or authority over the lands. What is peculiar to American Sāmoa in comparison with any other jurisdiction in America is the hybrid legal system; the burden of proof rests with the *āiga* to prove their occupancy, cultivation, and authority over the lands. Not long ago, all lands were held as communal native lands. The pendulum has now swung so far to the other direction that the burden of proof for ownership rights now rests on the *āiga*. They must show their ancestral ties to communal lands to prove their own occupancy and cultivation.

The *mātai* possesses dominion, authority, and stewardship over the communal lands only if he or she holds the *mātai* title by consent of the *āiga* (*Talala v. Logo*, 1 A.S.R. 165 (1907)). Acts of dominion and authority over communal lands are not only forms of possession; they are inherent to the *fa'amātai* and *fa'asāmoa* systems. Native lands can be purposely left untouched and unassigned to *āiga* members by the authority of the senior *mātai* and village council. Under the Naval Administration, however, lands that were left virgin, without an individual occupying the land and evidencing "dominion over it," were reduced to a "virgin bush land" classification by the High Court. This "virgin bush land" classification assumes that it is without Sāmoan ownership (Coulter 1957, p. 87).[1]

What the High Court failed to recognize is that native lands also included unassigned lands that were unoccupied and uncultivated, possibly due to low population count or in deference to cultural considerations.

While the High Court correctly recognized that land in customary ownership is not permanent and can have fluid occupancy, some Sāmoan traditions purposely leave "virgin bush lands" unoccupied and uncultivated. For example, in Sāmoan custom, guesthouses and sleeping quarters of senior *mātai* title holders and their *āiga* are built on communal lands. These structures give notice to neighboring villages that certain *āiga* have claimed such lands under the senior *mātai* title holder. Native lands were assigned to be left open for such accommodations within the villages. In addition, senior *mātai* title holders and their *āiga* are buried on communal lands, and a certain amount of lands were purposely kept uncultivated for burial purposes. *Malagas* that were performed in the early 1900s required *malae* (vast open space) for visiting villages, dignitaries, and guests. There is no good comparison between western and Sāmoan traditions in terms of the exercise of authority and dominion over the lands. Western law expects to find an individual who is visible and physically exercising dominion over the lands to claim ownership. Yet, in Sāmoan tradition, there are ancient understandings that large tracts of communal lands can go uncultivated and unused for decades. Ownership and authority over them is held under the *fa'asāmoa*, with senior *mātai* assigning different land parcels for specific purposes.

Ancient Statute of Merton

The early naval jurists failed to consider the roots of English property rights and ownership when applying and using common law property rights in American Sāmoa. The legal presumption of individual ownership of lands in American Sāmoa is based on the eighteenth and nineteenth century English common law writings of William Blackstone and Henry Maine. The American Sāmoa High Court applied English common law with respect to property ownership without ever balancing custom, culture, and dissimilarities in law or environment. Individual land ownership did not exist at the beginning of English common law; there were, as dictated by the Ancient Statute of Merton, the English statute written by Henry III of England and the Barons, only estates of land (Ancient Statute of Merton 1811; ch. 4, vol. 143, 262). Fee simple and freehold types of land tenure were born from this older system. Landed estates were made available under the Crown to ensure that taxes were being collected by every Duke, Earl, Viscount, Baron, and vassal. Land ownership was not permanent, and the Crown did not award land in perpetuity. Power and control over the peerage system were developed to ensure the Crown had ultimate ownership of all land holdings, a key demonstration of economic domination over its subjects. Land estates were rewards to loyal subjects of the Crown, and military service (e.g., knighthood) was one way to demonstrate this loyalty. Anyone deemed an enemy of the Crown could be removed from the lands, stripped of noble title, have all their material wealth confiscated by the Crown, and even be imprisoned under a charge of treason. Land was not owned in perpetuity by any individual. Crown land was given and taken away as the monarchy saw fit.

USN commandants embraced the Black and Maine legal doctrine and Sāmoa's land decisions to validate the presumption that unoccupied native land, such as virgin bush land, belonged to no one. This presumption further opened the window of opportunity for anyone who cleared communal land as the first occupant to stake a right of claim. Justice Morrow's presumption that virgin lands belonged to no one was not applicable in England and it was not applicable in American Sāmoa either, for two reasons. First, in *fa'asāmoa* custom, all large and small tracts of land are communally held, whether the lands are occupied and cultivated or unoccupied and uncultivated. The High Court did not recognize these basic Sāmoan customs and ruled that land ownership rights could only be evidenced by a person visibly sitting on the land. Second, at the root of English common law there were only estates of land, not individualized land, so to conclude that unoccupied, uncultivated communal lands in American Sāmoa belonged to no one based on the English common law property rights is spurious at best. In fact, fee tail[2] and life estates[3] were prominently used in England to ensure the noble class's dominion and authority over the lands through the peerage system (Black's Law Dictionary 2001). The Crown extracted revenue and taxes for each parcel of crown land, with sunset dates to ensure estates were eventually returned to the Crown. This is a key difference between the English and the American Sāmoan systems; the High Court did not stop to consider or evaluate the potential long-term impacts of applying law derived from a peerage system on land ownership in American Sāmoa.

Case Law's Evolution from Adverse Land Rights to Individually Owned Land Tenure

In 1900, there were only two types of land tenure in American Sāmoa: freehold and native (communal lands). Figure 7.1 depicts how individually owned land was developed through adverse land possession principles by the High Court from 1901 through the 1980s.

Between 1901 and 1930, the High Court under various naval commandants allowed individuals to use adverse land possession rights to claim title over communal lands whose ownership was primarily evidenced by exclusive possession, control, and cultivation. These early cases were built on the premise that adversely possessing land didn't require customary collaboration or dialogue. It was applied to American Sāmoa simply because it was accepted in every other "civilized" place. In the 1930s, the criteria for adverse land possession evolved from exclusive possession and occupation to exclusive possession and cultivation. The new requirements favored the users' rights above all other considerations. USN Commandant Wood, more than any other commandant, considered indigenous oral history merely tradition (hearsay) and disqualified testimonial evidence in the High Court, thereby favoring users' rights.

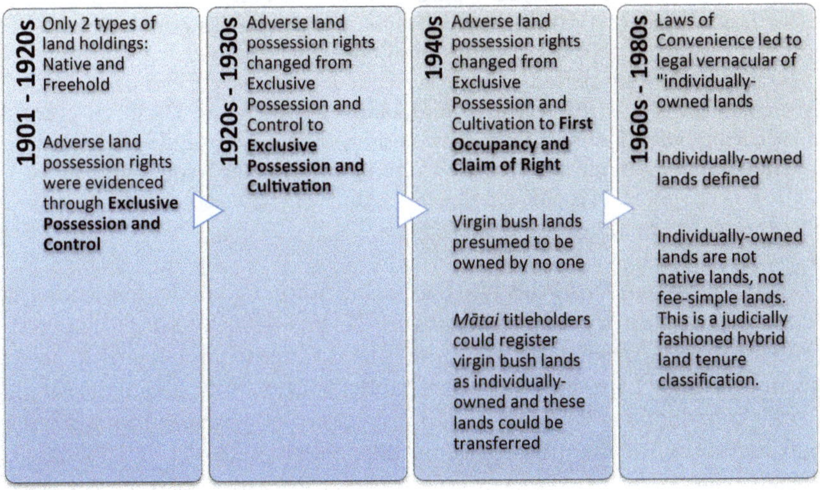

Fig. 7.1 1901–1980s, tracing adverse land possession rights into individually owned land tenure. Line-Noue Memea Kruse, May 2015

Oral Tradition Termed "Hearsay" and Oral History Limited to 40 Years

In the 1900s when the Naval High Court began hearing land disputes, they did so without recorded surveys, written deeds, or any form of written records of land ownership. Pacific Islanders passed down genealogy, legends, spiritual and cultural myths, taboos, and history of family lands through orature. The transition from orature to written language (Sāmoan and English) only came in the mid-1800s as the missionaries set up schools in the villages to teach Christianity and western behaviors and dress to the Sāmoans.

In order for a defendant to prove positive title against an adverse land possession claimant, the defendant needed to prove continuous possession and cultivation. Without written records, the High Court only had oral testimony of witnesses to determine land ownership rights. Since the High Court considered oral testimony (without written records) hearsay and therefore inadmissible as evidence, it had great difficulty handling land ownership disputes. Out of necessity, the High Court admitted some oral history (which typically would have been considered hearsay in America) but placed limitations on testimony based on the oral history of family lands. In *Tialavea v. Aga* the High Court stated:

> Most of the tradition was handed down orally—all of it orally for about 200 years for Samoans a good many years after the missionaries came to Samoa about 1830 [...] It is common knowledge that tradition handed down orally over a long period of time is frequently not very trustworthy. This elementary fact is the reason that tradition in one family about an event occurring years before is frequently entirely different from the tradition in another family about the same event. And the longer the tradition is handed down, the more it is subject to error. After all, tradition is only hearsay. (*Tialavea v. Aga*, 3 A.S.R. 272, 275 (1957))

USN Commandant Wood distrusted testimony given by Sāmoans that reported oral history of ancestry. After several years of conflicting testimony between families of the same and different branches of ancestral lineage laying claim on communal lands, Wood limited oral history of family knowledge in land ownership disputes to 40 years. Wood, obviously bewildered by the inconsistent testimony, asserts:

> I am willing to hear the history of this family as it bears upon this piece of land, but I am not willing to hear the history of this family just as history. The question is who owns this land Auau or Patea. However I am perfectly

> willing to listen to the history of the family, if the witness does not state what someone a long time ago said. In a *Mātai* name case I do not go back further than ten *Mātais*, which is never over 75 years, but in a land case 40 years is far enough. All I want to know is who has undisputed possession of this land for the past 40 years, which is twice the usual time of 20 years. If you cannot prove your case without going back several hundred years your case would not seem to be [a] strong one. I will only allow the family history as it pertains to this particular piece of land for the past 40 years. (*Patea v. Auvau*, 1 A.S.R. 380 (1926))

Oral history testimony was belittled as "pure tradition" by the USN commandants and an unacceptable form of evidence (*Tuiolosega v. Voa,* 2 A.S.R. 138 (1941)).[4] Due to case after case of conflicting testimony given by Sāmoan witnesses about ownership of land without any written record, the High Court limited oral history to 40 years. In *Tuiolosega v. Voa*, the plaintiff, representing himself, claimed that he cleared land called Mati on the island of Olosega in the Manu'a Group that was entirely bush and that he planted banana, manioc, coconuts, and *taro* and lived there for a long period of time (*Tuiolosega v. Voa,* 2 A.S.R. 138 (1941). The Letuli family, a branch of the Voa family clan, testified on behalf of the defendant to ownership and occupation and based their testimony on the word of their ancestors. The Letuli witness testified that prior to 1918, the Voa family had entered the bush land and planted fruits and took fruits upon their claim of ownership (*Tuiolosega v. Voa,* 2 A.S.R. 138 (1941). The High Court declared that the Letuli family exercised open, notorious, actual, visible, exclusive, continuous, and hostile occupation while under a claim of title before and since 1918. The Letuli family was awarded the land in Olosega because Justice Morrow determined their possession, which was testified to have continued for more than 20 years, was "clearly adverse to any claims to Tuiolosega or his family." Morrow specified that Tuiolosega's testimony was entirely "pure tradition" and that he had no personal knowledge as to the ownership of the land.[5] Most judges deemed pure tradition so convoluted that they did not permit testimony of genealogies to prove connection to communal lands. In *Vili v. Faiivae*, Gurr stopped witnesses from testifying about their genealogies because it was believed to be "pure tradition" (*Vili Siopitu Faatoa v. Faiivae*, 1 A.S.R. 38 (1906)). Disallowing testimony about genealogy, however conflicting such testimony was from opposing parties, severely limited the opportunity of witnesses to prove their genealogical connections to communal lands and the interconnections to the *mātai* structure that may have allowed them use and occupation of disputed lands. This was especially difficult during the 1800s because of the civil wars. In the Vili case, the defendant wanted to testify about families living on the lands during the Tualati-Lealatua war, but all oral history testimony was precluded by Gurr.

In *Tufaga v. Liufau*, the Naval High Court stressed that the testimony of both parties was founded solely upon pure tradition and that the High Court cannot favor the statement of one party over another. No party's claim was declared to have any solid foundation in fact (*Tufaga v. Liufau*, 1 A.S.R. 184 (1903)). Without written records and with conflicting testimonies about ownership of lands, the Naval High Court was often left to make assertions or assumptions about where and how the rule of law could be logically applied. In Tufaga, Morrow concluded that the merits of the adverse land possession were fully satisfied (*Tufaga v. Liufau*, 1 A.S.R. 184 (1903)). Although Tuiolosega adamantly testified that the original entry by Voa was unlawful and oppressive, the Naval High Court was confident that enough time had elapsed for the court to assume that Tuiolosega had acquiesced.

In *Letuli v. Faaea* the parties claimed ownership over Olosega lands called Falesamātai, which were composed of Falesama-Uta, Falesama-Tai, Fanuaee, Loíloí, and Taufasi. The defendant claimed that their ancestor Afe gave permission to Letuli to enter and use the lands for the past 20 years. Naturally, Letuli claimed his right to the land was not by permission but through a claim of ownership (*Letuli v. Faaea*, No. 8-1941). Morrow decided that the defendant's witnesses had no personal knowledge that Afe gave Letuli permission to enter Falesamātai, rendering the testimony as pure hearsay. Going even further, Morrow stated at the end of the testimonies that "Tradition in one family does not rise even to the dignity of reputation in the community as to the ownership of land" (*Letuli v. Faaea*, No. 8-1941).

1901–1930

In 1901, USN Commandant Tilley strongly laid out adverse possession rights in American Sāmoa through *Leiato v. Howden* to firmly establish the political sovereignty of the US territory as separate from Independent State of Sāmoa. Without mincing words, Tilley declared:

> The case before the court was of the greatest importance to all the people of Tutuila; that if this unproved claim of the chief in Upolu were admitted it

> must be upon the grounds of tradition or family stories; that such would involve nearly all the lands in Tutuila. That the government of the United States could not admit nor approve claims to lands in Tutuila by people in Upolu unless such claims be fully proved: that in the present case there was no evidence whatsoever [...] This case is one of the greatest importance, for the reason that it involves a claim to land by people who have not lived on the land for a long time. Included in the same class of claims are all the claims of the residents of Upolu claiming land in Tutuila. The court has found it imperative—absolutely necessary—to follow the practice that is general now in every civilized portion of the earth, and that is to recognize that the occupancy of the land for a fixed period, constitutes an ownership of the land (in this case 10 years uninterrupted occupancy). It is absolutely necessary, as I have said, that the government, through the court, shall take such extent to protect the natives of Tutuila, who have so long occupied the land, cultivated and improved it, from the onslaught of claimants from Upolu. (*Leiato v. Howden,* 1 A.S.R. 45 (1901))

Tilley clearly favored *mātai* titles in American Sāmoa over those from the neighboring lands of German Sāmoa. The newly formed High Court applied the principles of adverse land possession, but USN Commandant-Governor Sebree defined the period of occupancy for claiming a prescriptive land title was ten years prior to the land dispute.[6] This became the standard for all land title claims in American Sāmoa. In 1905, USN Commandant Moore defined exclusive and hostile possession in adverse land disputes. In *Sapela v. Mageo*, exclusive possession was defined as "a possession exclusive to all persons whatsoever," and hostile possession was "done or made in such manner and under such circumstances as to leave no doubt that they came to the knowledge of the owner or some one [*sic*] representing him" (*Sapela v. Mageo,* 1 A.S.R. 125 (1905). Moore also emphasized that although there may have not been written notice, there must have been possession so open and notorious it would raise a presumption of notice to him "equivalent to actual notice" (*Sapela v. Mageo,* 1 A.S.R. 125 (1905).

Also in 1905, USN Commandant Moore ruled in favor of the plaintiff in *Maloata v. Leoso*, declaring "that the Plaintiff has cultivated and improved the land permanently and has reaped the produce, the fruits of his labor" (*Maloata v. Leoso,* 1 A.S.R. 138 (1905)). Although just five years earlier all land was considered native lands, Moore declared that "It was a well known [sic] custom in Samoa that the **individual owner of property**, notwithstanding his well established rights to it, was subject to the will of the community and upon the commission of any act contrary to the desire of the community he would be banished or have to submit to gross degradation imposed by the people" (emphasis added) (*Maloata v. Leoso*, 1 A.S.R. 138 (1905). Moore may have based this assertion on a misinterpretation of the *mātai* title system, under which the individual has *pule* over the native lands at the will of the community. He may have understood "individual owner of the property" as meaning that the *mātai* title holder had authority at the will of the *āiga*, per the *fa'asāmoa* custom. The definition of "individual" in the Sāmoan context, however, is not analogous to the western definition. The *mātai* title holder is not perceived as an "individual" in the western sense because his authority and dominion over communal land is but a link in the Sāmoan customary chain of county chiefs, village council, senior *mātai*, orator, and *mātai* title holder. Moore introduced a legal term with specific meaning into the laws about land rights vested in an individual—an introduction which became a stepping stone on the path to recognizing individual rights to property.

Two years later, in 1907, Moore referenced his own decision and again applied the ten-year undisturbed adverse possession requirement in American Sāmoa. He justified the adverse principle and ten-year period by simply citing the rules of the Sāmoa Land Commission and Sāmoa's Supreme Court, which were created in the 1890 Tripartite Agreement. In *Pafuti v. Logo*, Moore emphasized that Logo had undisturbed possession and control from before Pafuti's 1883 arrival to the village of Aoa (*Pafuti v. Logo*, 1 A.S.R. 167 (1907). Significant in this ruling was the balancing of western law with *fa'amātai* and *fa'asāmoa*, because the plaintiff, Pafuti, was the daughter of Mata'afa. Mata'afa is a *Tamaāiga*,[7] title from the Independent State of Sāmoa. Pafuti stated in court that she was claiming the right of ownership to Aoa lands as the daughter of Mata'afa, and the court obliged her claim of right due to the *fa'asāmoa* custom with respect to this *Tamaāiga* title. Moore recognized her claim of right as an agent for Mata'afa. In communication with Mata'afa for this case, "by reason of courtesy to so high a chief, the question of Pafuti Talala's relationship was not allowed to be discussed in court, but she was accepted as Mataafa's agent" (*Pafuti v. Logo*, 1 A.S.R. 167 (1907). Although there was no recorded evidence of Pafuti's relationship to Mata'afa and no proof of Mata'afa's claim of title to land, the Naval Court nonetheless, based on Sāmoan custom, granted the plaintiff's case to proceed. Moore decided that Logo had undisputed possession and control of the lands in question from before 1883 when Pafuti entered Aoa. Moore went even further, stating that even if Mata'afa had certain rights upon Aoa and imposed a *sā*[8] (taboo or prohibition) on the lands (as testified by the plaintiff's witnesses) Logo never lost control or possession of the lands (*Pafuti v. Logo,* 1 A.S.R. 167 (1907). Logo openly disputed any rights or claims that Mata'afa from the Independent State of Sāmoa made to Aoa since before the new Government. Therefore, Moore granted Aoa to Logo and issued a strongly worded decision in favor of the possessor of lands:

> The possession of these lands by Logo and the people claiming with him, was open, exclusive, and continuous, so far as Mataafa was concerned, from the visit of Mataafa in 1883 to the visit of Pafuti Talala, as the daughter of Mataafa, in the year 1903 or 1906, which would make it more than twenty-two years between the two [sic] of any claim of Mataafa to the lands in question, and this Court cannot consider any secret, underhand communication with Mataafa as strengthening his right to hold these lands. It is not worth while [sic] for this Court to cite the numberless authorities on the question of the settlement of titles by adverse possession. The doctrine is so well understood that it is a waste of time to discuss it. (*Pafuti v. Logo,* 1 A.S.R. 167 (1907))

Between the 1920s and 1930s, the High Court's rules of evidence for adverse land rights evolved from exclusive possession and occupancy to exclusive possession and cultivation. Occupation evolved into cultivation. Cultivation became the new requirement to evidence adverse rights. Village ordinances imposed by the USN commandants, under penalty of hefty fines, required all individuals and *mātais* to cultivate *taro*, *ta'amū*, bananas, and coconuts. In 1926, Wood, openly critical of oral history as hearsay, proclaimed cultivation as key to adversely claimed land:

> In whichever one of these examples this particular case comes under, or any land case, it is not necessary to go back into the dim past to clear your title. You do not have to rely on stories that have been handed down in a family for ten generations to establish a title [...] In this particular case, I want to know who is taking care of the land, who is cutting the copra and living there, saying 'this is my land.' (*Patea v. Auvau*, 1 A.S.R. 380 (1926))

In 1930, the High Court also decided that to determine ownership of land, they must consider the *āiga* that took all produce and profits from the land for over 20 years (*Satele v. Afoa,* 1 A.S.R. 424 (1930)). In *Tuimalo v. Mailo*, the High Court stated, "The best evidence of communal ownership of land is clearing, planting, cultivating, and building upon the land" (*Tuimalo v. Mailo,* 1 A.S.R. 434 at 26 (1931)). While the requirement of cultivation replaced that of control, exclusive possession remained a steadfast requirement (*Talo v. Tavai,* 2 A.S.R. 63 (1938).

1930–1940

Without any US congressional oversight, commission, or agency to monitor whether the actions of the Naval Administration were within the promises of the two Deeds of Cession and within the spirit of the 1899 Treaty of Berlin, USN Commandants (concurrent judges and Governors) did next to nothing to research the negative impacts their decisions would have upon customary lands and traditions. While the Naval Commandants lacked consistency and long tenure on the bench, Justice Morrow was consistent in his decisions as the longest serving judge in the High Court—to the detriment of Sāmoan customary land tenure.

In the 1930s, exclusive possession and control continued to be upheld in court as the basis for adverse land possession claims, although the statutory period of 10 years changed to 20 years (*Talo v. Tavai*, 2 A.S.R. 64 (1938); *Salavea v. Ilaoa,* 2 A.S.R. 16 (1938)). These cases expressed the court's philosophy toward ownership of native land that marginalized Sāmoan custom. Morrow effectively defined and recognized "private land ownership" in American Sāmoa such that his approach did not appear to conflict the two Deeds of Cession. He even decreed private land ownership was within Sāmoan custom (*Talo v. Tavai*, 2 A.S.R. 64 (1938)). Morrow didn't provide any legal references for his brazen assertions that *fa'asāmoa* practiced private land ownership in some shape or form. Adverse land possession added the legal possibility of "individual" ownership to a system of land tenure classification that had previously only had categories of native and freehold. Prefatory right to individual ownership of land was recognized by the High Court as distinct and separate from the native or otherwise communal lands under the *fa'asāmoa* and *fa'amātai* structure. In 1933, in *Avegalio v. Suafoa*, three *āiga* members in the Leone district all claimed ownership to a specific parcel of land, which was quite small when compared to the communal land parcels that make up all of Leone (*Avegalio v. Suafoa,* 1 A.S.R. 476 (1932)). Each party in the Leone land dispute had conflicting names for the land. The first plaintiff (Avegalio) called it "Aupuga," the second plaintiff (Salave'a) called it "Mulivai," and the defendant called the land "Lalolasi." The different naming of lands by *āiga* clans continued throughout the first 50 years of the Naval Administration and largely ended after the Department of the Interior took over the administration of the islands. Salave'a testified that the land was owned by him as an "individual," not by *mātai* title rights or communally. He claimed it was "individual," not individually owned, because this land classification had not yet been created by the High Court. Salave'a testified that he had received the land as an individual, not a native, from his father Fepulea'i, and that Fepulea'i had received the land as an individual from his father, Su'a. USN Commandant Wood seemed to be taken back by this bold claim of "individual" ownership, because in court he proclaimed, "You know, do you not, that there is very little land owned in American Samoa by individuals, how did it happen that this land came to be owned by an individual" (*Avegalio v. Suafoa,* 1 A.S.R. 476 (1932)). In this case, the High Court again decided to split the land. Avegalio was entitled to the land west of the stream and north of the road passing through it to the northern boundary. Suafoa received the land in the *mātai* title solely because of his testimony that his *āiga* had an uninterrupted and adverse use of the land for at least 40 years, cultivating the land, while Salave'a had not possessed or cultivated the land for at least 20 years (*Avegalio v. Suafoa,* 1 A.S.R. 476 (1932)).

It was also at this time that Morrow stated that the High Court had determined the possession of land created presumption of ownership in the possessor (*Avegalio v. Suafoa,* 1 A.S.R. 476 (1932). In *Talo v. Tavai*, Morrow relied upon sixth century *Corpus Juris Civilis* (first codification of Roman and Civil Law), seventeenth century English statutes of adverse land possession rights in possessor and occupant, and early twentieth century work by real property scholar Herbert Tiffany. Taken together, these sources creatively devised limitations on how native land might be held under Sāmoan custom. Under Sāmoan custom, dispersed and low population numbers and large tracts of land with unassigned parcels would always make exclusive possession difficult to prove. Applying ancient western real property principles without carefully considering the long-term impacts to Sāmoan custom and native lands effectively rubber-stamped the Judge's "Laws of Convenience," giving weight to civil codes and laws that favored the possessor who is in "open, notorious, actual, visible, exclusive, continuous, hostile, and […] adverse possession."

In 1938, Morrow created individually owned right to land ownership in American Sāmoa. In the case of *Fa'aafe and Una'i v. Sioeli*, Morrow awarded individual land ownership through adverse possession to the plaintiffs as tenants in common. This decision to award individually owned land was entirely distinct from American Sāmoa customary law regarding native lands and the voiding of obligations of service to the *fa'asāmoa* and *fa'amātai* systems or the *mātai* title holders, village council, and *āiga*. Sioeli surveyed "Asiapa" land in Fagatogo and claimed that this land was not native land but individually owned, while the plaintiffs, objecting to his land registration, claimed Asiapa was individually owned by Fa'aafe and Una'i (*Faaafe v. Unai*, 2 A.S.R. 22 (1938)). Without having provided any factual or legal references in law, Justice Morrow declared that, based on the land surveys of Asiapa and both party's sworn testimonies, Asiapa was not native land but individually owned. The claim by both parties that Asiapa was individually owned outside of native lands is preposterous; in 1900, there was only native and freehold land tenure. Sioeli testified that approximately 60 years before the case was heard, Mailo had sold the land to Sioeli's father, Taeu Paea, and that upon his death, Asiapa was willed to Sioeli (*Faaafe v. Unai*, 2 A.S.R. 22 (1938)). This would mean that in 1878 Mailo sold "Asiapa" to Taeau Paea as individually owned land. This could not have happened in 1878 because there were only native lands in American Sāmoa at that time and a very select few parcels of freehold lands.

Morrow did not critically question Sioeli's testimony that the land was individually owned by his father or willed to him; he sidestepped these assertions altogether by deciding Sioeli's entire testimony was based on hearsay (*Faaafe v. Unai*, 2 A.S.R. 22 (1938)). How or why these lands were able to be converted into individually owned (rather than native) was never explicitly stated in court or through testimony of the witnesses. From 1900 to 1938, no single case ever explicitly defined or identified how, where, or why native lands were suddenly made into "private or individual" lands. There were only generalizations from the bench with strong affirmations that private ownership existed in Sāmoan custom. Morrow's presumption that private ownership existed in Sāmoan custom drove forward the widespread application of adverse possession of lands.

1940–1960

The 20-year period between 1940 and 1960 was a time of immense change to traditional customary land tenure in American Sāmoa. The previous three decades under the Naval Administration had provided the building blocks, but it was in this period that the concept of individually owned land was cemented. Virgin bush was legally defined as belonging to no one.

Between 1945 and 1947, the High Court placed the burden of providing positive title on the traditional *mātai* title holder to factually evidence occupation and claim of right. Prior to the Naval Administration, genealogical knowledge of *āiga* and their lands were all under the *fa'amātai* structure. Surveys were not needed because, like other indigenous cultures without written language, natural boundaries were used to distribute resources and demarcate land parcels. During this period, the High Court acknowledged that exclusive possession and cultivation were enough to adversely possess lands, cultivated or uncultivated. A series of cases starting in 1945 established a presumption that uncultivated virgin bush lands were "not native lands" and belonged to no one. This meant that all uncultivated and virgin lands were presumed to not be under the *fa'asāmoa* or *fa'amātai pule* (authority).

In the 1945 case *Tiumalu v. Lutu*, the High Court acknowledged the rights of individually owned land. Individually owned land was classified as distinct and separate from freehold land. This landmark case established the presumption of individual ownership, as well as the right for the property to be inheritable (*Tiumalu v. Lutu,* 2 A.S.R. 222, 224 (1945)). In Tiumalu, the court divided ownership of two pieces of land, Asi and Sigataupule, in Fagatogo village. Sigataupule land was awarded as individually owned to Lutu Simaile (the defendant), not through customary practices but through intestate succession of right through the defendant's deceased father, Afoa. In other words, the court granted the title vested in Lutu Simaile through inheritance. In contrast, Asi land was awarded to the plaintiffs as communally owned. The court acknowledged that, absent evidence of communal ownership, land could be defined as "individually, as opposed to communally, owned" (*Tiumalu v. Lutu,* 2 A.S.R. 222, 224 (1945)). This meant that if the parties in dispute claimed that these lands belong to no *mātai* or were not part of *āiga* lands—for example, virgin bush lands—the High Court may declare these lands freely available to become individualized. Here the Naval Administration opened the door to a form of alienation of lands; the ruling allowed individual Sāmoans to own land and did not proscribe a set of clear criteria to prevent the mass individualization of customary lands. The use of the term "alienation of lands" in this instance does not imply nationality or ethnicity; rather it is meant to highlight that the Naval High Court developed the alienation of communally owned lands (and virgin bush lands) among American Sāmoans. Without a clear set of criteria or parameters for individual ownership, the High Court's decisions during the 1940s directly led to the impossibility of communal lands being preserved in uncultivated large parcels for future generations.

Justice Morrow's decisions further laid the groundwork for individually owned land tenure. Several years later, in *Tago v. Mauga*, Morrow again made declarations about Sāmoan culture and land ownership without bothering to describe legal precedent or historical foundation, stating that "Samoans acquire title to bush land under custom by open occupation and use coupled with claim of ownership" (*Tago v. Mauga*, 2 A.S.R. 285 (1947)). Morrow did not provide specific details as to how bush lands were handled in terms of *fa'asāmoa* because all lands had originally been native. Morrow makes clear distinctions between bush lands and native lands; this action could arguably be described as him creating an "improper legal fiction." The legal fiction that "bush lands belongs to no one" is not based on factual foundation or legal justification. Morrow eagerly accepted Vaipito as individually owned land and gave Sami and Fa'afeu Mauga individual land rights based on testimony from persons such as Pulu and Soliai, who claimed that the previous *mātai* title holder Mauga Moimoi owned it individually and not through his paramount *mātai* title (*Tago v. Mauga*, 2 A.S.R. 285 (1947)).[9] Morrow expanded the alienation of lands, by ruling that land could be freely willed to his heirs, his adopted daughters Sami and Fa'afeu (*Tago v. Mauga*, 2 A.S.R. 285 at 7 (1947)). In his opinion, Morrow accepts the testimony on behalf of Sami and Fa'afeu Mauga that Mauga Moimoi entered Vaipito while it was bush land "owned by no one" and that he acquired title to it through first occupancy and claim of right (*Tago v. Mauga*, 2 A.S.R. 285 at 2 (1947)).

There was no reconciliation by the High Court between the western principles of first occupancy and claim of right and the *fa'asāmoa* custom and system of native land tenure. Both the High Court and Morrow mention briefly the fact that Sāmoan custom does in fact address first occupancy and claim of rights, but neither discuss these elements of custom or tradition, and not once in any of his cases does Morrow provide the legal basis for how and when virgin lands became "owned by no one" within Sāmoan custom. Morrow declared that in Sāmoan custom, individual land ownership existed and then later without factual foundation declared that bush lands belonged to no one (*Talo v. Tavai*, 2 A.S.R. 64 (1938)). These High Court decisions created improper legal fiction to apportion communal lands and determined that bush lands are not under *fa'amātai* authority and stewardship. Not only is custom affected without the access and use of traditional native lands but the practice of and future of *mātai* is delimited.

Attributes of Individually Owned Lands

In 1948, Justice Morrow started to partially define individually owned land by attributing certain characteristics to that land classification. The *Fono* failed to vet the statutory language defining individually owned lands and failed to create mechanisms to monitor or regulate this type of judicially produced land tenure. In *Taatiatia v. Misi*, the High Court continued to declare that virgin bush land belonged to no one, applying the old English law of Blackstone and Maine to the American Sāmoan land system.

Justice Morrow didn't stop at defining virgin bush land as belonging to no one. He created new methods for converting land to individual ownership by ruling that individually owned lands could be created if a *mātai* gives them away as such (*Gi v. Taetafea*, 2 A.S.R. 401, 403 (1948)). He claimed that this had been done in the past by pronouncing, "We know judicially that some *mātai*s in American Samoa have, with the consent of their family members, given family lands outright to certain members of their families. Taetafea testified that she was present and heard old Gi in 1905 make a gift of this land to her and her husband and that such gift was a reward for splendid service rendered by her husband and herself to Gi; also that such gift was followed by possession by the donees" (*Gi v. Taetafea*, 2 A.S.R. 401, 403 at 10 (1948)). Morrow may have misunderstood or misinterpreted the context; the phrases "giving land outright" and "assigning land for particular family's use" might have referred to the Sāmoan custom of *fa'amātai* and communal land sharing among *āiga* through distribution and allocation.

Several weeks later, in *Muli v. Ofoia*, Justice Morrow decided that if virgin, unclaimed land is occupied and cleared for an individual's benefit, the High Court would determine this evidence sufficient to right of individual title ownership (*Muli v. Ofofia*, 2 A.S.R. 408, 410 (1948)). The twentieth century laws against the alienation of land were meant to stop foreigners from taking away native lands from Sāmoans; instead, native lands were being stripped from *fa'asāmoa* custom and apportioned by the Naval Administration through its improper legal fiction built upon their introduced "Laws of Convenience."

1960–1980

By the 1960s, individually owned land tenure had become firmly planted in the legal vernacular of American Sāmoan society. Sāmoans, both *mātais* and non-*mātais*, recognized that native lands could be turned into individually owned lands if an individual continued to adversely possess the land for a statutory period, or if an individual cleared virgin bush land, or if a *mātai* gifted the land as individually owned. These earlier cases were used as established precedent in cases of individually owned land rights, and together they outlined specific circumstances in which land title could be awarded to an individual.

In *Government v. Letuli*, the High Court awarded very large parcels of individually owned land on prime real estate near the airport by citing the earlier cases of acquisition of title by first occupancy and claim of ownership:

> This court has ruled many times that Samoans may acquire title to land through first occupancy accompanied by claim of ownership. Soliai v. Lagafua, No. 5-1949 (H.C. of Am. S.); Faatiliga v. Fano, No. 89-1948 (H.C. of Am. S.); Gi v. Te'o, No. 35-1961 (H.C. of Am. S.); Magalei et. al., Lualemaga et. al., No. 60-1961 (H.C. of Am. S.). This doctrine of the acquisition of title by first occupancy coupled with a claim of ownership is approved in Main's Ancient Law (3rd Am. Ed.) 238. See also 2 Blackstone 8. The most common way for a Samoan to acquire title to land is to clear a portion of the virgin bush, put it in plantations on the cleared area, and claim it as his own land or the communal land of his family. This is a recognized way of acquiring land of his family. This is a recognized way of acquiring land according to Samoan customs. (*Government v. Letuli,* LT No. 016-63 (1963))

The High Court again referred to Blackstone and Maine, utilizing the same irrelevant English philosophies to justify the individualization of land ownership in American Sāmoa. Earlier 1920s and 1930s court decisions had replaced exclusive possession and cultivation requirements with first occupancy and claim of right. After 60 years, the *Fono* finally tried to define individually owned lands, but it failed to pass by majority vote in two consecutive *Fono* sessions:

> Sec.9.0103—INDIVIDUALLY OWNED LAND: Individually owned land means land that is owned by a person in one of the first two categories named in Sec. 9.0102, or that is in court grants prior to 1900. Such land

> may be conveyed only to a person or family in the categories mentioned in Sec.9.0102, except that it may be inherited by devise or descent under the laws of intestate succession, by natural lineal descendants of the owner. If no person is qualified to inherit, the title shall revert to the family from which the title was derived.[10]

At least seven attempts to define individually owned lands never made it out of the first house.[11] As the *Fono* couldn't muster enough political will to define this judicially made land tenure, the High Court proceeded to craft its own definition.

In the 1974 case *Haleck v. Tuia*, the High Court expanded once again the definition of individually owned land rights by deciding that individual land rights are established when a person enters virgin bush land that no other person previously cultivated, provided that the first occupier clears the entire land "substantially," and a "considerable plantation was developed" (*Haleck v. Tuia*, LT No. 1384-74 (1974)). Still other possibilities for creating acceptable types of individually owned land registrations were discussed, including no objections being made to the registering of the land at the Territorial Registrar's office, an individual entering the land on other than the direction of *mātai*, the work being done entirely at the individual's expense, and the work being other than a "communal effort" (*Haleck v. Tuia*, LT No. 1384-74 (1974)). The High Court added another definition for individually owned land. Whereby previously the registrant needed to be the first occupant and establish a claim of right when clearing virgin bush land, in 1974, the court modified the claim of right, stating that it could be based on "substantially clearing the entire land." By this time in the late 1970s, individually owned land rights and the concept of private land ownership had fully taken hold within American Sāmoa.

The defining attributes and conceptual definition of individually owned land was built on precedent cases, and the 1977 *Fanene v. Talio* case perfectly reveals how individually owned tenure apportions the communal land system. The access and use of resources that had once been shared among neighboring *āiga* on contiguous parcels of land were forever disrupted. *Fanene v. Talio* was complicated because 11 cases were consolidated into one trial, some parties claimed sections of Malaeimi land as individually owned, others claimed sections as communally owned, several leases existed, and some parcels were large lands and others much smaller lands (*Fanene v. Talio,* LT 64-77, slip op. (Trial Div. April 22, 1980)). Fanene claimed 265.9 acres as individually owned although a major part of the entire acreage remained virgin bush. Fonoti claimed 35 acres ("Alatutui") as individually owned land based on adverse use of land for over 30 years and first occupant claims. Fagaima claimed 34 acres of individually owned land based on adverse possession of 30 years. Tauiliili claimed 24.40 acres of individually owned land through clearing virgin bush in its entirety and performing some cultivation. Sotoa claimed 21.15 acres of individually owned land entirely cleared by his father and cultivated and thereby demonstrating dominion over the land. Moeitai claimed 1 acre of individually owned land. Uiva Te'o claimed 79.86 acres as individually owned land on the extreme southwest portion of the Fanene lands called "Etena." Tuiaana Moi claimed individually owned lands through adverse possession and first occupant claims. Heirs of Niue Malufau claimed 12.55 acres and 18.015 acres. Fanene claimed lands of 265.9 acres. Leapaga claimed 4.37 acres of land ("Lepine") as communal property. One of the rulings by the High Court in the 11 consolidated cases decided in favor of Fagaima, who was declared the individual owner of the 34.04 acres of land against Fonoti, Tauiliili, and Sotoa *āiga*. Fagaima's winning claim shows how 34.04 acres were forever destructured from the total 265.9 acres that once were used by the Fanene *āiga*.

The Malaeimi land parcels were divided among *āiga* clans and made into individually owned lands with surveyed boundaries and amended maps, all registered with the Territorial Registrar. Most of these land parcels were individualized because of the 1960s cases that established first occupancy and claim of right as elements for establishing individual ownership, and the other cases were individualized by outright adverse possession or by clearing virgin bush land in its entirety. On appeal, Justice Richard I. Miyamoto described individually owned land as that land:

> (1) cleared in its entirety or substantially so from the virgin bush by an individual through his own initiative and not by, for or under the direction of his aiga or the senior *mātai*, (2) cultivated in its entirety or substantially so by him, and (3) occupied by him or his family or agents continuously from the time of the clearing of the bush. (*Leuma, Avegalio, etal. v. Willis,* LT 47-79, slip op. (Land and Titles Div. Dec. 16, 1980))

Justice Miyamoto's ruling has become the leading case on defining individually owned land rights. This case set the scene "how to convert and register" bush lands into individually owned lands, sidestepping the *Sa'o* and *fa'amātai* since 1977. Justice Miyamoto introduced a lower standard for individualized land by stating that the land could be cleared substantially and not necessarily in its entirety. The path to individual ownership once again opened even wider.

Growth of Individually Owned Lands

In a modern, moneyed economy, some traditional aspects of Sāmoan custom have changed with respect to communal lands. War over land and power has been replaced with war in the courts. The American Sāmoa Land and Titles Court is made up of laws, statutes, and regulations that are only partly in accordance with Sāmoan custom.

Substantial distinctions between Independent State of Sāmoa and American Sāmoa Land and Titles Court make land and *mātai* title disputes that cross the two jurisdictions noteworthy. In American Sāmoa, land and *mātai* title cases are brought before the Land and Titles Court with lawyers to present the case to the judges. In Independent State of Sāmoa, Western-trained barristers are not permitted to present land and *mātai* title cases. For both American Sāmoa and Independent State of Sāmoa, the difficulty in resolving land and titles disputes without the traditional means of dialogue and/or threat of war required a new system. Independent State of Sāmoa created the Land and Titles Court, which was effectively a hybrid system that accommodated both Sāmoan culture and custom and Western democratic jurisprudence. In the Land and Titles Court, land and *mātai* title cases are brought before the court not by barristers but by individuals in dispute. Barristers are not permitted to speak on behalf of any claimant in the Land and Titles Court. Judges have no law degrees but are appointed because of their expertise with Sāmoan culture, genealogy, land, history, oratory, and language skills.

In American Sāmoa, all land and titles disputes are first heard at the local government level with the Office of Sāmoan Affairs. The Office of Sāmoan Affairs acts as a neutral third party to resolve disputes. The parties in dispute must meet with the Office of Sāmoan Affairs at least two times before going to the Land and Titles Court. American Sāmoa's Land and Titles Court has formalized the American jurisprudence of law: attorneys represent disputing parties in front of Western-trained judges accompanied by several Sāmoan judges, a remnant of the Naval past when all Chief Justices were foreigners and needed experts of land and *mātai* to assist them in adjudicating land and titles cases (*Leiato v Howden*, 1 A.S.R. 149 (1906)).[12]

Notes

1. "There is, however, no written evidence of the ownership of forest lands, and the court bases its decisions of ownership of such lands largely on their use. That is to say, if a piece of forest land has been cleared and used for four or five years and is then surveyed and registered, the registration is likely to be uncontested. If it is contested, the asserted historical circumstances of family ownership will count for something, but actual use of the land by another family is a weightier consideration."
2. Fee tail is an estate that is inheritable only by specified descendants of the original grantee, and that endures until its current holder dies without issue.
3. Life estate is an estate held only for the duration of a specified person's life, usually the possessor's.
4. In *Levale* et al. *v. Toaga*, No. 26A-1945, Justice Cyril Wyche stated, "The question of title to real estate in American Samoa is always a difficult one to solve for the reason that in most cases there is no recorded title to, nor description of property. Title to real estate is generally proved by family tradition."
5. Justice Morrow referenced in this case, *Talo v. Tavai*, 2 A.S.R. 63 (1938); *Letuli v. Faaea,* No. 8-1941 in which title to land cannot be evidenced by hearsay. There is no such exception to the hearsay rule, also referencing *Howland v. Crocker*, 7 Allen (MASS.), 153; *South School District v. Blakeslee*, 13 CONN. 227, 235.
6. Ten years became the precedent to adversely claim land, see *Tiumalu v. Fuimaono*, 1 ASR 17 (1901); *Laapui v. Taua*, 1 ASR 25 (1901), *Mauga v. Gaogao*, H.C. LT 2-1905, *Pafuti v. Logo*, 1 ASR 166 (1907).
7. *Tamaāiga* is the equivalent of a "royal" title.
8. *Sā* when used in this context means forbidden or out of bounds.
9. Pulu first testified that he was familiar with the land since he was a *mātai* title holder in the Mauga *āiga*, and he was 70 years of age and had a very long history to the lands in general, and then he stated that the Vaipito belonged to Mauga Moimoi as an individual. However, after a court recess he changed his testimony that Mauga Moimoi did not own the land as an individual. However, Judge Morrow refused to rescind his original testimony and believed his original testimony was more accurate in that Mauga Moimoi owned the land as an individual.
10. Act of April 7, 1962, Pub.L.7-19, codified IX Code American Samoa, section 9.0103 (1961). According to Article I, Section 3 and Article II, Section 9, Rev. Const. Am. Samoa, this legislative bill must pass two successive legislatures for it to be enacted into law.

11. S.107, 15th Fono, 3d Sess. (1978); H.157, 15th Fono, 3d Sess. (1978); H.220, 15th Fono, 4th Sess. (1978); S.2, 16th Fono, 1st Sess. (1979); S.59, 16th Fono, 2nd Sess. (1979); H.119, 16th Fono, 2nd Sess. (1979); S.97, 16th Fono, 3d Sess. (1980).
12. *Leiato v Howden*, 1 A.S.R. 149 (1906).

References

Avegalio v. Suafoa, 1 A.S.R. 476 (1932).

Craddick v. Territorial Registrar of American Samoa, CA 61-78, slip op. (Trial Div. May 10, 1979) (Order Denying Motion for New Trial or Rehearing Civil Action No. 61-78).

Faaafe v. Unai, 2 A.S.R. 22 (1938).

Fanene v. Talio, LT 64-77, slip op. (Trial Div. April 22, 1980).

Gi v. Taetafea, 2 A.S.R. 401, 403 (1948).

Government v. Letuli, LT No. 016-63 (1963).

Haleck v. Tuia, LT No. 1384-74 (1974).

Howland v. Crocker, 7 Allen (MASS.), 153.

Laapui v. Taua, 1 A.S.R. 25 (1901).

Leiato v. Howden, 1 A.S.R. 45 (1901).

Leuma v. Willis, LT 047-79, Slip op. at 4 (Land and Titles Div. Dec. 16, 1980).

Levale et al. v. Toaga, No. 26A-1945.

Letuli v. Faaea, No. 8-1941.

Maloata v. Leoso, 1 A.S.R. 138 (1905).

Mauga v. Gaogao, H.C. LT 2-1905.

Muli v. Ofofia, 2 A.S.R. 408, 410 (1948).

Pafuti v. Logo, 1 A.S.R. 166 (1907).

Patea v. Auvau, 1 A.S.R. 380 (1926).

Salavea v. Ilaoa, 2 A.S.R. 16 (1938).

Sapela v. Mageo, 1 A.S.R. 125 (1905).

Satele v. Afoa, 1 A.S.R. 424 (1930).

South School District v. Blakeslee, 13 CONN. 227, 235.

Tago v. Mauga, 2 A.S.R. 285 (1947).

Talala v. Logo, 1 A.S.R. 165 (1907).

Talo v. Tavai, 2 A.S.R. 63 (1938).

Tialavea v. Aga, 3 A.S.R. 272, 275 (1957).

Tiumalu v. Fuimaono, 1 A.S.R. 17 (1901).

Tiumalu v. Lutu, 2 A.S.R. 222, 224 (1945).

Tufaga v. Liufau, 1 A.S.R. 184 (1903).

Tuimalo v. Mailo, 1 A.S.R. 434 at 26 (1931).

Tuiolosega v. Voa, 2 A.S.R. 138 (1941).

Vili Siopitu Faatoa v. Faiivae, 1 A.S.R. 38 (1906).
Ancient Statute of Merton 1811; ch. 4, vol. 143, 262.
American Sāmoa Government Department of Commerce. *Statistical Yearbook* 2013. Published Annually. http://www.doc.as.gov.
BLACK'S LAW DICTIONARY. 2nd ed. (2001).
Coulter, John W. 1957. *The Pacific Dependencies of the United States*. New York: Macmillan Company.

CHAPTER 8

Retention of Communal Lands

Protection Mechanisms and Failures for Communal Land Tenure

Deeds of Cession which require, among other things, "respect and protect[ion …] of all people dwelling in Tutuila to their lands," and that the rights of "all people concerning their property according to their customs shall be recognized" (A.S.C.A. sec. 2 (1981) [48 U.S.C. § 1661]). The Revised Constitution of American Sāmoa mandates a policy of protective legislation, which requires the courts to interpret statutes in a way that is protective of the Sāmoan custom. Articles I and III state in relevant parts:

> It shall be the policy of the government of American Sāmoa to protect persons of Sāmoan ancestry against alienation of their lands and destruction of the Sāmoan way of life.

Additionally, Article I, section three, and Article II, section nine, of the Revised American Sāmoa Constitution require that any bill proposing a change in the law respecting the alienation or transfer of land be passed by two successive legislatures by a two-thirds vote of the entire membership of both houses.

Despite all the customary land preservation mechanisms, there is still opportunity for mischief under the current registration statutes. Currently the protective mechanisms are statutes regulating the alienation of lands

L.-N. Memea Kruse, *The Pacific Insular Case of American Sāmoa*,
https://doi.org/10.1007/978-3-319-69971-4_8

(A.S.C.A. § 37.0201 et seq. (1999)). Not only has the High Court allowed individualized holding, but the *Fono* has also made the individualization process relatively easy by passage of the Land Registration Act. This Act provides:

Registration—Absence of conflicting claim a prerequisite.

1. The owner of ***any land*** in American Sāmoa not previously registered may register his title thereto with the Territorial Registrar.
2. No title to land shall be registered unless the Registrar is satisfied that there is no conflicting claim thereto and unless the description clearly identifies the boundaries of the land by metes and bounds.
3. Every registration shall specify whether the land is registered as family owned communal land or ***individually owned*** land.

In other words, any individual can register a claim to "any land [...] not previously registered," which comprises majority of land in the territory, if no one objects in 60 days. Such title registration has been consistently upheld by the courts. Anthropology professor Walter Tiffany suggests this title registration of native lands leads to individual ownership by effectively "individualiz[ing] land rights and confer[ring] security of tenure against other descent group members" (Tiffany 1981, pp. 136–153). Through this registration process, the Territorial Registrar has registered individual title claims to uncleared and uncultivated bush land. Tiffany prophetically asserts that "whether the people of American Sāmoa wish to see their traditional land tenure patterns so affected, only they can say." In other words, when the local people determine what type of future they want to have, they will be able to influence the furthering and lessening of protections to traditional land.

Since individual land tenure was created by the courts without any territorial input or legislative discussion, a few jurists eventually used it to qualify individual ownership elements of land tenure. The American Sāmoa Code Annotated (ASCA) is silent on the issue of individually owned lands. Individually owned land was born from a series of judicial decisions allowing for this classification of land based upon continuous occupancy and cultivation (*Alesana v. Siupolu*, 1 A.S.R. 346, 351 (1922)). The Naval jurists expressly relied upon the doctrine in Herbert T. Tiffany's *The Law of Real Property and Other Interests in land* and Henry S. Maine's *On Ancient Law: Its Connection with the Early History of Society, and Its Relation to Modern Ideas (1864)* which Associate Justice Thomas Murphy extensively cites in *Taatiatia v. Misi Taatiatia v. Misi,* 2 A.S.R. 346 (1948). In *Taatiatia,* Justice Morrow took from *Maine* and *Tiffany* the concept of individual right to land (*Maloata v. Leoso,* 1 A.S.R. 134, 138 (1905); *Satele v. Afoa,* 1 A.S.R. 467, 471 (1932)). In *Aleona v. Suipolu,* the Naval jurists implied the title or individual right to land and then steadily built the doctrine upon with successive cases (*Alesana v. Suipolu,* 1 A.S.R. 346 (1922); *Maloata v. Leoso,* 1 A.S.R. 134, 138 (1905); *Satele v. Afoa,* 1 A.S.R. 467, 471 (1932)). In 1948, Morrow, in *Taatiatia v. Misi,* espoused how a claim of right under "individually owned land" may be granted for virgin lands using the law of old England. Chief Justice Morrow stated:

> It is our conclusion from the evidence, which in some respects is conflicting, that Misi entered upon the land in 1919 while it was bush and cut the large trees thereon and that after letting the trees lie for a year he burned them and proceeded to put in plantations, and that he has used the land ever since for plantation purposes. The land being bush and not occupied by anyone was *res nullius,* the property of no one. When Misi entered upon it and cut down the trees and put in his plantations and claimed the land as his own, it became his in accordance with the customs of the Sāmoans, which customs, when not in conflict with the laws of American Sāmoa or the laws of the United States concerning American Sāmoa, are preserved. Sec. 2 of the A.S. Code. There is no law of American Sāmoa or of the United States concerning American Sāmoa in conflict with the customs of the Sāmoans with respect to the acquisition of title to bush land. Blackstone considered that an original title to property was acquired by the first occupant under a claim of ownership. (*Taatiatia v. Misi,* 2 A.S.R. 346 (1948))

Thirty years later, Justice Murphy, hearing the appeal on *Leuma v. Willis* and obviously unimpressed with Judge Morrow's overview of Sāmoan traditional customary land usage in *Taatiatia v. Misi,* criticized Morrow's opinion as misinterpreting Sāmoan custom (*Leuma v. Willis,* LT 047-79, slip op. at 4 (Land and Titles Div. Dec. 16, 1980)). Murphy disagreed with Morrow's view that virgin bush belongs to no one and averred that Morrow was misapplying the law of old England to a completely different land system and culture. In the dissent in *Taatiatia,* Appellate Justice Murphy questioned Morrow's application of Blackstone and Maine in American Sāmoa. Justice Murphy obstinately quips, "It seems Justice Morrow misstated Samoan custom (that virgin bush belonged to no one), and then applied the law of old England (Blackstone and Maine) to a land system and culture completely different. It is no wonder he got such a result as the concept of homesteading individually owned land" (*Leuma v. Willis*, LT 047-79, slip op. at 9 (Land and Titles Div. Dec. 16, 1980)).

The common law of England was introduced into most of the countries in the South Pacific during the period of colonial expansion. Cook Islands, Niue, Sāmoa, and Tokelau were acquired as dependencies of the British colony of New Zealand. New legislation stated that colonial outpost lands were vested in the British Crown.[1] Tonga followed suit in its Constitution of 1875, which states that "All the land is the property of the King" (Tonga Constitution (1875) §104). The common law of England was readily used as authority for enlightened western law and civility in the South Pacific region.

Law in a Christian Context

The core problem with Morrow's application of the *Commentaries* by Sir William Blackstone to incorporate the concept of individual land ownership is that the political philosophy precepts are born from the belief in a Christian God. This assumes two things: there is only one god, and all men are Christian. Blackstone's *Commentaries Book 2* is taken in part from the works of Cicero, where the focus is upon the individual man ("Blackstone's Commentaries" 2014, website). In England, Blackstone's *Commentaries* were used like a code, providing ammunition in the creation of legislation, a movement toward clearer and more substantive English law (Cairns 1984, p. 4).

In the Enlightenment era, Europeans were beginning to defy the notion that Kings and Queens were earthly representatives of God. Enlightenment thinkers proposed that men are individuals with natural born rights, while the French later addressed the rights of women. Enlightenment writings ground the absolute rights of individuals in Christian scriptures and thought, which hold that the omnipotent Christian creator gave to man "dominion over the all the earth; and over the fish of the sea, and over the fowl of the air, and over every living that that moveth upon the earth" ("Blackstone's Commentaries" 2012, website). English law and Christianity were intertwined, but in American Sāmoa the traditional religion has many gods and the culture is founded on the family and village. The question here of whether the English concept of individual and natural rights is acceptable in different religious and if cultural contexts needs to be addressed.

The application of the Blackstone *Commentaries* to delineate land ownership in American Sāmoa based on the notion of the "individual" is completely incongruent with the underlying cultural and religious backbone of this Polynesian society (Kamu 1996).[2] Through the gradual imposition of foreign land principles, the Naval Administration promoted concepts of property based on principles of natural justice expressed in English common law. Concepts of law and society prioritized the expression of the individual over the rights of the community, which took the form of family and village. Colonialist attempts to promote economic and social development throughout the world were based on this privileging of the rights of the individual (Hooker 1975). Classic legal pluralism is the outcome of a colonial encounter in which a Western colonial body of law incorporates an indigenous/ customary body of law (Hooker 1975). University of Kent at Canterbury law professor Michael Hooker suggests that since the absorption of the indigenous body of law is always achieved from a place of power, the status and dominion of this body of law is determined by "legal arrangements controlled by the colonial authorities," a subservient position vis-à-vis the dominant position of the Western body of law (Sahar 2012, p. 134). Hooker's theory suggests that these identified set of norms are controlled by the state and in the case of American Sāmoa—by the Naval Administration (Sahar 2012, pp. 290–298). The Court, an appendage of the state, exerted its civilizing influence through the authority of law, which led to the acceptance of Western land concepts within Sāmoan societies.

Keeping Land in Sāmoan Hands

In 1962, the *Fono* passed laws recognizing the concept of individually owned land without defining it, but restricted its ownership to: (1) a full blood[ed] American Sāmoan or (2) a person who is of at least one-half Sāmoan blood, was born in American Sāmoa, is a descendant of an American-Sāmoan family, lives with Sāmoans as a Sāmoan, has lived in American Sāmoa for more than five years, and has officially declared his intention to make American Sāmoa his home for life (A.S.C.A. § 37.0201 (1999) and 37.0204 et. seq. (1982)). Associate Judge Miyamoto in December 1974 defined individually owned land as follows:

> land (1) cleared in its entirety or substantially so from virgin bush by an individual through his own initiative and not by, for, or under, the direction of his aiga or the senior *mātai*, (2) cultivated in its entirety or substantially

> so by him, and (3) occupied by him, or his family, or agents continuously from the time of the clearing of the bush.[3] (*Fanene v. Talio*, H.C., LT. No 64-1977)

The 1979 Economic Development Plan for American Sāmoa (FY 1979–1984) recognized the threat and trend of individually owned land interest over the traditional communal land concept:

> Because most communal land has not been surveyed and registered, portions of 'neglected' communal land holdings which had not been developed or cultivated are susceptible to encroachments by Sāmoans seeking individually owned native land through homesteading, as well as by members of neighboring aigas who have settled on land without knowing the boundaries of adjacent communal lands. Increasing numbers of such cases are being adjudicated by the High Court of American Sāmoa. As a result, some communal landowners are beginning to feel that property rights must be diligently protected **since the law recognizes the forfeiture to others when such lands are not utilized by communal landowners** (emphasis added). ("Economic Plan for American Samoa" 1980)

The group that authored the 1979 Economic Development Plan was composed of traditional leaders, *mātai*, and local business owners. They recognized the threat that individually owned land posed to communal land tenure and argued that communally held lands must be protected from this introduced "homesteading" practice. It was believed at that time, based on the analysis of the Department of Commerce Territorial Planning Commission, that the transfer of communal native lands to individually owned native lands had increased for several reasons, including:

1. A growing minority of Sāmoan families desire to break away from the communal obligations that are required of those who settle on communal land.
2. Individual members of a family do not have perpetual rights to communal lands; therefore, the acquisition of individually owned land would assure that property and land could be willed to their children or other heirs.
3. Individually native land is an acceptable form of collateral for obtaining home and business loans. ("Economic Plan for American Samoa" 1980)

The growth at that time of communal lands converted to individually owned lands seems to reflect a more Americanized lifestyle, one free from village obligations. Land ownership enabled private property to be freely used and willed to heirs.

The earlier 1969 Economic Development Plan for American Sāmoa, drafted by Washington DC consultants under contract to the US Economic Development Administration, describes individually owned lands as a non-threat and praised the work of the US Navy administration protecting local customs by "recognizing the importance of communal land and traditional systems of land tenure" in American Sāmoa ("economic development program" 1969, p. 160). There were no interviews, surveys, or quantifiable data analyzed or conducted by this east coast consultant to measure how the Navy commandants were protecting customs, communal lands, and traditional systems of land tenure. The Navy introduced adverse possession concepts and principles without considering the parameters, limitations, or impact upon an indigenous culture. Also, disastrous to the traditional communal lands was the desire of some Sāmoans to will privately held land to their heirs and take advantage of financial opportunities for individual land owners to invest in residential, commercial, and industrial development in American Sāmoa ("Economic Plan for American Samoa" 1980). The longest serving Chief Justice of the High Court of American Sāmoa, Arthur Morrow, declared:

> In view of the fact that the US Supreme Court has ruled a number of times that racially discriminatory laws are unconstitutional, it would follow in all probability that our racially discriminatory land law would be held unconstitutional and Americans could come here with plenty of money and buy up Sāmoan land. The Sāmoans would use the money to buy pisupo. [a]utomobiles and take trips to the States. In the end, the Sāmoans would not have their land, the pisupo, or [sic] the money and the automobiles would wear out. They would be in the same situation that the Hawaiians were in when they lost their land. (Morrow 1974, pp. 14–15)

American Sāmoa "Native" Definition

The American Sāmoa *Fono* also has had a role in defining who is eligible to own land. According to the ASCA Title 27 section 201, the definition of a native Sāmoan is "a full-blooded Sāmoan," and a non-native Sāmoan is "any person who is not a full-blooded Sāmoan" (A.S.C.A. § 37.0201

(1999) and 37.0204 et seq. (1982); *Moon v. Falemalama*, 4 A.S.R. 836 (1975)). Thus, a native Sāmoan was defined as a full-blooded individual regardless of citizenship. This meant that Sāmoan citizens (Independent State of Sāmoa) who were full-blooded Sāmoans were legally recognized as natives of American Sāmoa and permitted to own land. Conversely, any individual living in American Sāmoa who was not a full-blooded Sāmoan was alienated from land ownership. Because of this, the *Fono* changed the definition of "native" in 1982, restricting the definition of native to "a full-blooded Sāmoan person of Tutuila, Manu'a, Aunu'u or Swains Island" (A.S.C.A. 37.0204, readopted 1980; PL 16-88 §§ 1, 2). Essentially, the *Fono* narrowed the parameters of what it meant to be an American Sāmoan native and legally excluded any Sāmoan outside the territory, specifically Sāmoan citizens (Independent State of Sāmoa). Nationality became a determining factor in who could be legally recognized as a native and, therefore, entitled to ownership of lands in American Sāmoa. To date, the *Fono* has not established regulations regarding individual land ownership.

The increase in individually owned lands does not only impact the communal establishment within a village unit. This type of private land ownership also limits the access to and use of natural flora, fauna, water, and food resources for cultural purposes, not to mention contributes to the destruction of the few precious rainforests in American Sāmoa. On April 11, 2008, the American Sāmoa Government (ASG), Department of Commerce, and American Sāmoa Coastal Zone Management Program (CZM) sought a permanent injunction against a family from what the ASG believed to be the last remaining rainforest area in Tafuna being cleared for development (*American Sāmoa Government v. Haleck*, LT 10-08, slip op. (Trial Div. May 1, 2013)). A family claimed approximately 26 acres of land as "individually owned land" simply by registration through the Territorial Registrar's office without any signs of human habitation, development, or continuous occupation required by law. The family sought to clear and develop the last Tafuna rainforest for commercial purposes based on their assertions that these lands were registered as individually owned lands. On May 1, 2013, the High Court ruled in favor of ASG for permanent injunction relief. The ruling declared that the rainforest "is, to overstate the obvious, forested—a diametrically opposed set of defining characteristics to land that has been *cleared, cultivated, and occupied*" (*American Sāmoa Government v. Haleck*, LT 10-08, slip op. (Trial Div. May 1, 2013)). The High Court took a strong position and set a precedent that individuals cannot simply claim rainforest in American

Sāmoa by cutting some trees down and registering it as individually owned land. The High Court clearly states that "A proposition that rainforest land can be individually owned is plainly nonsense; the two are logical contradictions." The High Court specifies that no one can "obtain title to lands as his or her individually owned land simply by registering title with the Territorial Registrar." The High Court identified that for someone who has procured a registration of land as individual ownership, the subject land must have been:

> (1) *cleared* in its entirety or substantially so from the virgin bush by an individual through his own initiative and not by, for or under the direction of his aiga or the senior *mātai*, (2) *cultivated* in its entirety or substantially so by him, and (3) *occupied* by him or his family or agents continuously from the time of the clearing of the bush. development. (*American Sāmoa Government v. Haleck,* LT 10-08, slip op. (Trial Div. May 1, 2013))

The family in this case cited adverse possession entitlements, specifically cutting virgin bush and continuous occupation which enabled their alleged right to claim individually owned lands. During the trial, the High Court emphasized the importance of this rainforest, citing the delicate balance of the island's ecosystem containing indigenous trees, *manuma* (colored fruit dove), *manutagi* (purple cap fruit dove), and *lupe* (Pacific pigeon). Scientists provided evidence no other forest in the lowland area exists that can support these types of indigenous flora and fauna. In *Sese v. Leota* (1988), *Fania v. Atualevao* (1990), and *Manoa v. Jennings* (1992), the courts have advocated for a restriction of the individually owned lands and for more restrictive regulations that should be implemented by the *Fono* (*Sese v. Leota*, 9 A.S.R. 2d 25, 26-27 (1988); *Fania v. Atualevao,* 14 A.S.R. 2d 70, 72 (1990); *Manoa v. Jennings*, 21 A.S.R. 2d 23, 24 (1992)). The High Court concluded that the public good is served by the preservation of the rainforest, "the public's interest will not be disserved by preservation of the lowland's sole primary forest that contains many of this island's unique species of trees, birds and bats. In fact, the public's interest would only be furthered by the protection of the Rainforest."[4]

Efforts to Retain Customary Land and Mātai *System*

University of Hawai'i at Mānoa law professor Jon Van Dyke aptly describes the unique relationship the United States has with each of these five island communities, American Sāmoa, Guam, Puerto Rico, Commonwealth of

Northern Mariana Islands, and the Virgin Islands as defined by a matrix of "individualized laws" that has no discernible legal foundation or precise framework yet established each political affiliation or territorial status (Laughlin 1995, pp. 505–510). In the *Leneuoti Fiafia Tuaua* et al. *v. United States of America*, the Appeals Court stated, "…the Court has continued to invoke the Insular framework when dealing with questions of territorial and extraterritorial application. Although some aspects of the Insular Cases' analysis may now be deemed politically incorrect, the framework remains both applicable and of pragmatic use in assessing the applicability of rights to unincorporated territories."

With a precise framework supporting a political and legal status, each political jurisdiction knows exactly why and how to be accepted into the US political body. Both parties can forecast how long this union will benefit both sides based on the mutual understanding of why the amalgamation was favored in the first place. The primary purpose of the arduous Sāmoan struggle is the retention of its customary tenure of lands and *mātai* system. Both political science professor Norman Meller from the University of Hawai'i at Mānoa and emeritus Pacific Islands studies professor Donald Denoon of Australian National University have articulated some of the challenges: how Pacific communities negotiate who is indigenous, how to seek self-determination, and how to achieve such goals within the political hodgepodge tapestry of decolonized states in the Pacific Ocean (Meller 2000, pp. 1–19). Former Governor Peter T. Coleman (the first Sāmoan Governor) stressed that without the *mātai* system and customary land tenure, the Sāmoan culture would be lost. The commonality among all the territories discussed previously is the convergence of customary practices and imported laws and rules and how they considerably changed under foreign occupation. The practice of territories (once foreign lands) becoming fully incorporated into the US body-politic as happened with the Northwest Territory, Alaska, and Hawai'i is not likely to be enacted for the current five US territories, even after more than 100 years of unincorporated status. Each jurisdiction faces diverse areas of promise and challenge; for American Sāmoa, the most important of these is customary land tenure and the *mātai* system. Sāmoan judges without legal training or law degrees, who are considered experts on custom and tradition, are appointed to the High Court and assist in cases on areas of customary law (A.S.C.A. § 3 et seq.; also, in *In re Mātai Title La'apui*, 4 A.S.R. 2d 7 (1987)). This practice in the American Sāmoa High Court is an example of the convergence of the practice of Western law and Sāmoan culture. This is a meaningful organizing principle for how Sāmoan customary law changes to meet the changing circumstances under Western law as a US territory.

In the last 114 years, a plebiscite has never been put on the ballot—instigated by the public or the *Fono*—to request the local Constitution change the land tenure system to grow the economy. Even with the dwindling educated and skilled workforce and recent economic shocks to the territorial economy, the customary land tenure system is highly valued by the people of American Sāmoa as the centerpiece of its culture.

Unanswered Questions

The Naval Administration introduced the "Laws of Convenience" as the standard of western, meaning American, property rights. Such laws were thought to symbolize American Sāmoa's acceptance of "civilization" and democracy in the Pacific. The "Laws of Convenience" introduced the concept of individual rights to land ownership, which led to the individually owned land classification. As early as 1907, the Navy was working actively to stabilize land titles in American Sāmoa, since the High Court perceived the native land and linkages to *fa'asāmoa* as being based on uncertainty and unqualified title ownership (*Talala v. Logo*, 1 A.S.R. 166, 171 (1907)). Slowly but steadily gaining momentum and force over the decades, the individual notion of private ownership distinct and separate from communal land holdings took shape, and by the 1980s, the criteria required to individualize land became more relaxed and therefore easier to prove in the High Court. It is remarkable that after 110 years of territorial status the *Fono* has never passed legislation to regulate or even to define this judicially manufactured land tenure. Over the last 60 years, the High Court succeeded in defining land tenure and remaking it by expanding and narrowing its parameters without objections or delimitations by the legislative branch.

Unfortunately, the individually owned land tenure classification does little to address the conundrums and challenges that led to land laws meant to protect native American Sāmoans from the alienation of their lands. Is the owner of individually owned lands the owner of the land in perpetuity? Individually owned land is not completely fee simple because it is conditioned upon at least one-half native blood. Communal land, by law, is only able to be owned in individual ownership if the owner is at least one-half native blood. This begs the question, if no one in government is monitoring individually owned land ownership and individually owned land growth, then how is the government properly enforcing the prevention of alienation of lands by ensuring the owner is at least one-half native blood as prescribed by law?

If the heir to individually owned land is less than one-half native blood, what happens to the individually owned parcel of land? If heirs to individually owned land are not one-half native blood, as required by statute and there are no governmental agencies to declare the lands inalienable, then happens to these land parcels?[5] If the heirs to individually owned land are less than one-half native blood, does the government have the right to revoke the registered lands because the owner has violated the alienation land laws? If this is the case and the government revokes the registered land, who is vested with the ownership rights upon revocation? Does the land parcel go back to the original *āiga* clan, the county council, or the Land Commission to decide (A.S.C.A. §37.02)?

The only way to solve these conundrums, as the High Court has recommended repeatedly, is for the *Fono* to institute parameters and definitions, thereby addressing these issues through the proper branch of government. Action through this branch also will permit direct democratic participation of constituents in the decision-making process addressing individually owned land tenure.

Notes

1. Cook Islands Act 1915 (NZ), sec. 354; Sāmoa Act 1921 (NZ), sec. 268; Tokelau Amendment Act 1976 (NZ), sec. 20; exception to land ownership were freehold and customary lands.
2. Lalomilo Kamu provides the pre-Christian concept of God from the Sāmoan perspective: "The question whether the Sāmoan views of the self-existent god Tagaloa have any bearings on the Christian views of God needs to be recognized. Based on the biblical traditions, God as the Christians believe, was there in the beginning. His word was the agent of his creation and nothing was created without him. He is the source and the creator of all things including 'man.' He is known as the God of creation; the God of Israel and he is also known as the national God of Israel even if God could never be nationally limited as such. From the Sāmoan creation story, god Tagaloa lives in the distant space or space beyond or in the sky (*vanimonimo/vateatea*). He was simply there in the beginning; the origin of the being was not the concern of the story. The details of the two creation stories are naturally not similar as they were evolved and developed from the life experience of the different people."

3. See also *Fonoti Aufata v. Heirs of Niue Malufau*, et al., H.C., LT. 60-1977.
4. Avamua Dave Haleck appealed this court case and the Appellate Division of the High Court ruled in Haleck's favor because the American Sāmoa Government prematurely applied for injunctive relief without first issuing a stop order, sanctions for such activity, and an administrative notice for public hearing. The Appellate Division therefore dissolved all injunctions and vacated all orders. Haleck is now free to apply again for a Land Use Permit and Project Notification and Review System to develop in this low-lying rainforest. See *Haleck v. Am. Sāmoa Gov't,* AP 06-13, slip-op. at 16 (App. Div. Aug. 16, 2014).
5. In 1962, the American Sāmoa *Fono* (legislature) passed laws recognizing the concept of individually owned land without defining it but restricted its ownership to: (1) a full blood[ed] American Sāmoan or (2) a person who is of at least one-half Sāmoan blood, was born in American Sāmoa, is a descendant of an American Sāmoan family, lives with Sāmoans as a Sāmoan, has lived in American Sāmoa for more than five years, and has officially declared his intention to make American Sāmoa his home for life, see ASCA §37.0201 (1999) and §37.0204 et. seq. (1982).

References

A.S.C.A. sec. 2 (1981) [48 U.S.C. § 1661]).

A.S.C.A. § 37.0201 et seq. (1999).

A.S.C.A. § 37.0204 et. seq. (1982).

A.S.C.A. 37.0204, readopted 1980; PL 16-88 §§ 1, 2.

Alesana v. Siupolu, 1 A.S.R. 346, 351 (1922).

American Sāmoa Government v. Haleck, LT 10-08, slip op. (Trial Div. May 1, 2013).

Fanene v. Talio, H.C., LT. No 64-1977.

Fania v. Atualevao, 14 A.S.R. 2d 70, 72 (1990).

Haleck v. Am. Sāmoa Gov't, AP 06-13, slip-op. at 16 (App. Div. Aug. 16, 2014).

Leuma v. Willis, LT 047-79, Slip op. at 4 (Land and Titles Div. Dec. 16, 1980).

Maloata v. Leoso, 1 A.S.R. 134, 138 (1905).

Moon v. Falemalama, 4 A.S.R. 836 (1975).

In re Mātai Title La'apui, 4 A.S.R. 2d 7 (1987).

Satele v. Afoa, 1 A.S.R. 467, 471 (1932).

Sese v. Leota, 9 A.S.R. 2d 25, 26–27 (1988).

Manoa v. Jennings, 21 A.S.R. 2d 23, 24 (1992).

Taatiatia v. Misi Taatiatia v. *Misi,* 2 A.S.R. 346 (1948).

Tonga Constitution (1875) §104.

"Blackstone's Commentaries on the Laws of England." In Book the Second—Chapter the First: Of Property in General, Yale Law School. Avalon Project. http://www.avalon.law.yale.edu/eighteenth _century/blackstone_bk2ch1.asp.

Cairns, John W. 1984. "Blackstone: An English Institutist: Legal Literature and the Rise of the Nation State." *Oxford Journal of Legal Studies* 4: 318.

Cortes, Antonio. 1987. Land in Trust: The Invasion of Palau's Land-Tenure Customs by American Law. *Asian-Pacific Law & Policy Journal* 14 (3): 167–240.

"Economic Plan of American Samoa." 1980. Report. Pago Pago: American Sāmoa.

"Economic Development Program." 1969. Report. Pago Pago: American Sāmoa.

Hooker, Michael. 1975. *Legal Pluralism: An Introduction to Colonial and Neo-Colonial Laws.* London: Oxford University Press.

Kamu, Lalomilo. 1996. *The Samoan Culture and the Christian Gospel.* Apia: Western Samoa.

Laughlin, Stanley K. 1995. *The Law of United States Territories and Affiliated Jurisdictions.* Eagan: Lawyers Cooperative Publishing.

Meller, Norman. 2000. "Indigenous Self Determination and Its Implementation." *Pacific Studies* 23 (1/2): 1.

Morrow, Arthur. 1974. *My thirty-two Years in American Samoa.*

Sahar, Ido. 2012. "Legal Pluralism Incarnate: An Institutional Perspective on Courts of Law in Colonial and Postcolonial Settings." *Journal of Legal Pluralism* 65: 133–163.

Tiffany, Walter W. 1981. "The Applicability of Western Judicial Concepts to Polynesian Land Disputes: High Court Use of the Adverse Possession Principle in American Sāmoa." *Oceania* 52 (2): 136–153.

U.S. Government Accountability Office GAO-12-798T. 2012. Report. "COMPACT OF FREE ASSOCIATION: Proposed U.S. Assistance to Palau through Fiscal Year 2024."

United Nations. *UNdata.* http://data.un.org/CountryProfile.aspx?crName=palau#Economic. Accessed 2 February 2015.

CHAPTER 9

Legal and Political Futures for American Sāmoa

Se'i fono le pa'a ma ona vae

American Sāmoa's legal and political relationship with the United States is currently being re-examined due to the growing number of off-island American Sāmoans wanting automatic US citizenship. Many on-island American Sāmoans maintain the century-old fear that automatic citizenship will result in the US Constitution being applied in its entirety to the territory and that the application of due process protections of the United States. The federal Constitution may invalidate the American Sāmoan Constitution. This would remove the express protections for communally owned lands that limit them exclusively to American Sāmoans. This chapter will identify the political and legal relationships with other territories, affiliated, and compact states to analyze political routes that could expand American Sāmoa's self-autonomy and preserve communal land tenure while upholding Sāmoan culture.

Independent State of Sāmoa (Sāmoa), Palau, and Mariana Islands can be compared for their similar, although not parallel, political status and histories that have intersected at times with the history of American Sāmoa. Table 9.1 illuminates the different relationships that each Pacific Island jurisdiction has with the United States.

Sāmoan proverb that means let the crab take counsel with its legs, which means one should think things out before taking action.

L.-N. Memea Kruse, *The Pacific Insular Case of American Sāmoa*,
https://doi.org/10.1007/978-3-319-69971-4_9

Table 9.1 Comparative political differences and similarities, 2015

	Citizenship	*Federal financial aid ($ in millions)*	*Congressional representative*	*Political status*	*Protections to land tenure*	*Access to United States*	*Eligible to conduct foreign trade/taxes*	*Member states of UN*
American Sāmoa	US national status (not US citizen)	$515 (direct economic assistance through Department of the Interior—FY 2010)	Non-voting delegate	Unincorporated/unorganized US territory (1900 and 1904 Deed of Cessions, Instrument of Political/Legal relationship with US) The United States provides defense and is solely responsible to conduct foreign trade Administers its own immigration and customs	Yes, in local Constitution	Unrestricted access	No Under US Internal Revenue Code	N/A
CNMI	US citizen	$250 (direct economic assistance through Department of the Interior—FY 2013)	Non-voting delegate	Commonwealth Covenant (Instrument of Political/Legal relationship with US) The United States provides defense and hybrid of sovereign/not sovereign. On May 8, 2008, the Consolidated Natural Resources Act of 2008 (CNRA) extended most provisions of US immigration law to the Commonwealth of the Northern Mariana Islands (the CNMI) for the first time in history. The transition period for implementing US immigration law in the CNMI began on Nov. 28, 2009, and is now scheduled to end on Dec. 31, 2019.[a] Administers its own customs	Yes, in Commonwealth Covenant	Unrestricted access	Yes. Under US Internal Revenue Code	N/A

(*continued*)

Table 9.1 (continued)

	Citizenship	*Federal financial aid ($ in millions)*	*Congressional representative*	*Political status*	*Protections to land tenure*	*Access to United States*	*Eligible to conduct foreign trade/ taxes*	*Member states of UN*
Palau	Palau citizen (not US citizen)	FY2011—FY2024: direct economic assistance ($107.5 million) for Palau government operations; infrastructure project grants ($40 million) to build mutually agreed projects; infrastructure maintenance fund ($28 million) for maintaining the Compact Road, Palau's primary airport, and certain other major US -funded projects; fiscal consolidation fund ($10 million) to assist Palau in debt reduction; and trust fund contributions ($30.25 million) in addition to the $70 million contributed under the compact[b]	N/A	Compact of Free Association (Instrument of Political/Legal relationship with US) The United States provides defense. Administers its own immigration and customs	Yes, in Compact of Free Association	Citizens of Palau by birth, and citizens of the former TTPI (Trust Territory of the Pacific Islands) who acquired Palau citizenship in 1994, are entitled under the Compact to travel and apply for admission to the United States as non-immigrants without visas[c]	Yes. Palau Island treated as foreign country for tax purposes and are eligible for the foreign-earned income exclusion	Member state

(*continued*)

Table 9.1 (continued)

	Citizenship	*Federal financial aid ($ in millions)*	*Congressional representative*	*Political status*	*Protections to land tenure*	*Access to United States*	*Eligible to conduct foreign trade/taxes*	*Member states of UN*
Sāmoa	Sāmoa citizen (not US citizen)	N/A	N/A	Sovereign country	Yes, in Constitution	Considered foreign country, must have Sāmoa passport	Yes. N/A	Member state

[a]US Citizenship and Immigration Services, *US Immigration Law in the Commonwealth of the Northern Mariana Islands (CNMI)*, website accessed January 1, 2016

[b]Government Accountability Office, GAO-12-798T. "COMPACT OF FREE ASSOCIATION: Proposed US Assistance to Palau through Fiscal Year 2024"

[c]US Citizenship and Immigration Services, *Federated States of Micronesia, Republic of the Marshall Islands, and Palau*, website accessed January 1, 2016

Other Political Frameworks in the Pacific Region

Independence: Independent State of Sāmoa

In 1962, Sāmoa was the first Pacific Island country to achieve independence. Sāmoa is a Westminster parliamentary democratic country and a model country for other Pacific Island states during an era of formal decolonization in the Pacific. It was categorized as a least developed country (LDC) by the United Nations in 1971 because it produced the lowest indicators of specific criterion for poverty, human resource, and economic vulnerability. In 2014, the United Nations graduated Sāmoa from LDC to developing country (DC) status, making Sāmoa only one of four countries to graduate to DC status in 43 years (US GAO 2012).

Sāmoa consists of 1090 square miles covering nine islands, with Savai'i (660 square miles) being the largest. Upolu (430 square miles), which hosts the capital Apia, is the second largest. The four main islands lie between 13 and 15 degrees south latitude and between 171 and 173 degrees west longitude. The 2015 population estimate for Sāmoa is 193,483, with 157,527 residing in the rural areas and 35,957 residing in urban areas (Sāmoa Bureau of Statistics 2011). Sāmoa is approximately 76 miles east southeast from American Sāmoa.

Mālo (National Government)

The 1962 Constitution of Sāmoa is derived from Great Britain's parliamentary democracy but was amended to enshrine national protections for Sāmoan customs. This parliamentary democracy provides for a head of state, prime minister, and cabinet. At the time of the Constitution's enactment, the heads of state (*O le Ao o le Mālo*), selected from among the *Tama-a-Aiga*, were given lifetime appointments. In the intervening years, this policy has changed, and terms in office are now proscribed.[1] Sāmoa's Constitution is distinguished from those of constitutional monarchies in that a simple majority vote may amend it. The prime minister is chosen by a majority in Parliament every five years. The Cabinet, ranging in members from 8 to 12, are appointed by the Prime Minister and sworn in by the Head of State. The Human Rights Protection Party (HRPP) is currently the majority party and holds all Cabinet seats, but it faces formidable opposition in Parliament, most notably from the Tautua Samoa Party, formerly known as the Samoan Democratic United Party.

The national government (*mālo*) is intertwined with the Parliament under its Parliamentarian democratic model. The unicameral legislature, *Fono Aoao Faitulafono* (National Legislative Assembly), is composed of 47 *mātai* members and two non-*mātai* members that serve five-year terms and must be Sāmoan citizens. The 47 *mātai* are elected from ethnic Samoan constituencies; the other two are chosen by the Samoan citizens on a separate "individual roll." These two seats are reserved for freehold land owners.[2] The Legislative Assembly is formed by the majority power, executive power is exercised by the *mālō*, and legislative power is vested with the Legislative Assembly. The intertwining of the *mālō* and Assembly results from the *mālō* control over legislation through its majority in the Legislative Assembly. The Judiciary branch is independent. Sāmoa's Constitution protects the culture, as does the Constitution of American Sāmoa, by requiring that only those within the *fa'amātai* system, or *mātai* title, may vote and stand as candidates in parliamentarian elections.

Mātai title holders who are Members of Parliament serve dual roles. In the village, they serve the family from which the title originates, and in Parliament they represent the area in which they are elected. Under the Electoral Amendment Acts of 1990 and 1991, all adult citizens may be eligible to vote in the constituency by residence, service, or via family connections. Voting in constituencies where there is a connection by residence means that if a citizen resides in one village but has a *mātai* title from another village, he or she may vote where the *mātai* title originates from. This electoral methodology recognizes the *fa'amātai* system by prescribing voting rights based on *fa'asāmoa* connections.

Local Government

Many of Sāmoa's civil and criminal matters are dealt with by *Fono o Mātai* (village councils) according to customary law, a practice further strengthened by the 1990 Village Fono Law.[3] The 1990 Village Act provides for the village *fono* to promulgate rules, punishment, and arbitration within the confines of the village. The village mayor (*pulenu'u*) is nominated by the village council but paid by the local government to liaise with government officials. The village mayor is not a career servant but is part of the local government structure, with responsibility for reporting on matters in the village and receiving assistance from the local government when necessary (Sui O Le Malo Act 1978).

Sources of Law: Customary Law and Western Law

The sources of law are found in the Constitution, statutes, English common law, and Sāmoan customary law (which are protected in the Constitution). The Constitution expressly prohibits the alienation of customary land beyond limited lease or license, and it may not be amended except by two-thirds majority in a referendum of territorial electors and then only if the Legislative Assembly has amended the Constitution through proper procedures and channels (Constitution of Independent State of Sāmoa art. IV, C(1)(c)). Otherwise, there is no delimiting of customary lands. Articles 100 and 101 of the Constitution expressly provide for custom and usage as a source of law in several important ways to protect the *fa'asāmoa* culture. *Mātai* titles and customary land are required to be "held in accordance with Samoan custom and usage." The Land and Titles Court was created to address *mātai* disputes and customary land interests (Sāmoa Land Titles Registration Act 2008).

Land and Titles Court

The Land and Titles Court has exclusive jurisdiction over custom and customary land disputes, and there is no codification of customary law. Land and Titles Court decisions provide the description and parameters of customary land matters (Constitution of Independent State of Sāmoa art. 101; Sāmoa Land and Titles Act 1981). *Pule* over the land through the *fa'amātai* system is assigned under custom and tradition by the *mātai* and *āiga*. Sāmoan judges are *mātai* and appointed for three-year terms. They are selected based on ability, character, standing, and reputation, and appointed by nomination of the Judicial Service Commission. The appeals process is limited to this court, and no further appeals are heard once the appeal has been decided (Sāmoa Land Titles Registration Act 2008).

Land Tenure and Governance

Customary land, freehold land, and public land are the only types of land tenure in Sāmoa. Freehold land is privately owned, public land belongs to the government, and customary land cannot be sold or mortgaged. Both customary and public lands may be leased.

Eighty percent of the land in Sāmoa is customary, 16 percent is freehold, and four percent is public. Customary protections against the alienation of land are firmly entrenched in the Constitution; these protections were fiercely sought and hard won during its drafting due to gluttonous land claims made by foreigners in the mid-1800s (Constitution of

Independent State of Sāmoa arts. 101 and 102). Only a resident Sāmoan citizen may own freehold land; potential landowners who are ineligible as a resident must obtain consent of the Head of State (Alienation of Freehold Land Act 1972 §2). The Alienation of Freehold Land Act of 1972 established a system that required the Head of State's written consent for any transfers of freehold land to companies where more than 25 percent of the shares are owned by foreigners, non-resident Sāmoan citizens, and individuals who are not Sāmoan citizens. These mechanisms restrict the transfer of freehold land to foreigners, foreign-owned companies, and non-resident Sāmoan citizens. Customary lands cannot be alienated.

Compact of Free Association: Republic of Palau

The Republic of Palau (Palau) is a vast archipelago of 343 islands with 188 square miles of land and a population of 21,000. It is situated seven degrees north of the equator and 134 degrees east longitude. Palau is an independent country that has a free association with the United States and is a UN-mandated Trust Territory of the United States. The "Free Association" term refers to the negotiated Compact terms, whereby the United States committed to Palau's self-governance in accordance with the freely expressed wishes of the Palauan people. This "territory" status is not to be confused with American Sāmoa's territory status; this categorization is a specific designation under the UN Trusteeship Agreement that authorized the United States "full powers of administration, legislation, and jurisdiction" over Palau (1947 United Nations Trusteeship art.3). In 1947, during the era of decolonization, the UN Security Council under the umbrella of the strategic Trusteeship Agreement (TTPI), mandated and enumerated the United States' specific responsibilities to provide for the development and promotion of self-sufficiency or independence should Palau's constituency desire it.

The UN sought the Trusteeship System following the defeat of Axis powers, and agreements were negotiated with individual countries to oversee the administration of territories once held under the Axis rule. In 1945, the UN Trusteeship System provided for:

1. Territories held under Mandates established by the League of Nations after the First World War
2. Territories detached from "enemy States" as a result of the Second World War

3. Territories voluntarily placed under the System by States responsible for their administration. (United Nations Charter chapt. XII, art. 77)

The UN felt that the Trusteeship System was needed to assist colonies of former Axis countries in achieving economic and social progress, and ultimately, self-determination. It was through the UN Charter that humanitarian principles were woven into the fabric of these newly created Trust Territories. For Palau to be placed under the US Trusteeship, fundamental freedoms were guaranteed.

At the Constitutional Convention in Washington DC, both the Mariana Islands (which will be discussed later) and Palau took their own delegation parties to negotiate terms with the United States after the 1975 plebiscite gave them Commonwealth status. The plebiscite validated the constituencies' desire to end the Trusteeship and begin the process of self-determination. The Micronesian states demanded separate status talks and forced the United States to concede to their terms. On the eighth plebiscite in November 2013, the Palauan constituency, by a 68 percent vote, ended the Trusteeship relationship with the United States and emerged in October 2014 as self-governing. Palau is now a self-governing independent country and the 185th member state of the UN.

Palau adopted its Constitution in 1981. The following year, after seven previous failed referendums, it signed the Compact of Free Association (COFA), PL 99-658, with the United States. The COFA granted the United States the right to take as much as one-third of the islands' lands for military bases. The citizens of Palau favored COFA only to repossess their indigenous lands from the public trust system that had been forced upon them, first by Japan and later by the United States. Under the Registration Act, Palau's National Code declared that all land in Palau can be owned only by citizens of Palau. Corporations owning land must also be wholly owned by Palau citizens (Palau National Code Title 39). The language within the Code provides authority to the Palau Government to reclaim any lands that were wrongfully taken under the Spanish, German, and Japanese colonial administrations, as well as the right to return these lands to the original owners (Palau National Code Title 39). The COFA gave Palau full domestic autonomy and allowed for foreign affairs and military protections in "free association" with the United States. Under the agreement, the United States assumes complete responsibility for the military and defense over Palau until 2031. In 1993, Palau held its eighth referendum on a general ballot that resulted in a majority vote in favor of the COFA.

National Government

Palau operates as a presidential representative democratic republic with a Constitution and a tripartite government consisting of separate executive, legislative, and judicial branches. There are currently no registered political parties; while parties have existed intermittently in the past, none have had staying power. The Legislature, *Olbiil era Kelulau*, is made up of two chambers, each with 25 members serving four-year terms. Palau has 16 states, and with one delegate elected from each state. Each delegate and Senator must be a citizen of Palau (Constitution of Palau art. IX).

Local Government

No statutory determination of authority or official intergovernmental relationship has been granted to Palau's Council of Chiefs. The Council is only an advisory committee, and it consults with the President about traditional laws, customs, and its impacts on the laws and Constitution.

Sources of Law: Customary Law and Western Law

Palau finds its sources of law in the Constitution, statutes (Palau National Code), and English common law. The Constitution is the supreme law of the land and does not expressly direct jurisdiction between customary law and statutes (Constitution of Palau art. II). The Supreme Court has not yet determined when the National Code and traditional law conflict with legal authority (Palau National Code Title I, §302).

Despite Palau's numerous colonial administrators since the late 1790s and its arduous path to self-governance, Palau has slowly reclaimed its indigenous lands. Spain took control under Pope Leo XIII in 1885 following the Spanish-American War. In 1899, Spain sold Palu to Imperial Germany administered as part of German New Guinea. Japan conquered Palau during World War I and following World War II Palau was placed under US-TTPI in 1947.

Land Tenure and Governance

Prior to foreign encroachment, lands were held communally and overseen by traditional leaders to provide for family clans in non-permanent usage. When Germany and Japan held administrative control over Palau, indigenous lands were forcibly or coercively taken, either by sale or by governmental procedure to declare the indigenous landowner's rights null and void. As a result, when the United States took over administration under the Trusteeship, all public lands became de facto American lands (Meller 2000). By 1935, as much as 84 percent of Palau indigenous lands belonged to the government under various state policies that stripped indigenous peoples of customary land use and ownership (Cortés 1987, p. 16). This type of action is well known in the Pacific: government lands are earmarked for military buildup, thereby displacing indigenous peoples, dismantling culture, apportioning and converting customary family lands into private ownership.

Palau has only two land tenure types: custom and freehold. The Palau National Code provides for freehold lands to be sold, leased, or conveyed as the owner desires. Foreigners cannot own land (Palau National Code Title 39). Leases over government and freehold lands cannot extend past 99 years. The preservation of communally owned lands was the basis of the Commonwealth Freely Associated State's pursuit for self-governance. The Palauan government negotiated under the COFA for a decentralized system of governance to maintain internal harmony among the states. The American State Department "Micronesian staffer" failed to create a more pro-American system of stronger centralized federal governance. This failure was so spectacular that the staff was disallowed from attending the last half of the Convention negotiations; it was obvious to Palauan representatives that the State Department was being too influential. Staffers passed notes such as this:

> Every effort should be made to assure that the convention does not write constitution containing clauses which would be seriously inconsistent or in conflict with an acceptable (to the U.S.) future political relationship [...]. The U.S. quietly should seek to work with the constitutional convention in identifying and avoiding problem areas which could later jeopardize negotiations of a satisfactory political relationship. (Cortés 1987, p. 110)

Palau's Senator Lazarus Salii went on record as saying that:

> Some staff members [...] have enormous emotional investments in the outcome [...] and preconceived ideas of what the outcome ought to be. The staff are not here to mastermind the Convention, not here to direct or steer us. They are here to render professional services. If they cannot give us their services without promoting their emotional and philosophical considerations, they should and this Convention should—reconsider their position. (Cortés 1987, p. 110)

Palauans established a federal presidential republican form of democratic governance, in which the states have local self-governing powers. The self-governing framework provides for more tradition and custom to be used under the Palau National Code to determine land tenure rights with the traditional leaders in every jurisdiction.

Under the COFA, from 1994 to 2010, Palau was given direct assistance of $15 million each fiscal year in addition to infrastructure assistance, valued at approximately $900 million ("Compact of Free" 2012). In 2011, under the COFA, assistance was slated to decrease by $215 million from FY 2011 to FY 2024. The forecasted decrease in assistance was important to note in the COFA arrangement, because greater financial independence from the national tax base translates into greater autonomy.

Commonwealth Covenant: Commonwealth of Northern Mariana Islands (CNMI)

The Mariana Islands group stretches across 16 islands with 184 square miles of land. The 2010 US Census records the population at 53,833, the majority of which is housed in Saipan. The indigenous people of the Northern Mariana Islands are the Chamorros, who are believed to have originated from Southeast Asia and arrived in the Islands in 1500 BC. Under Spanish rule, the Chamorros were forcefully relocated to Guam, which opened up their lands to Caroline Islanders to resettle and populate.

Between 1565 and 1978, the Mariana Islands were under the control of Spain, Germany, Japan, and the United States. Spain first colonized the islands in 1565 AD. Pope Leo XIII officially declared sovereignty over the Northern Mariana Islands in 1885. In 1899, following its defeat, Spain sold the Island chain to Germany, which ruled over the Islands until 1914. Between 1914 and 1944, Japan controlled Mariana Islands and from 1944 to 1947, the US Navy seized control. In 1947, it emerged as a "strategic trust." The UN Trusteeship Agreement authorized the United States to administer the Northern Mariana Islands. The Northern Mariana Islands was divested from the Department of State in 1962, and full authority and powers were transferred to the Department of the Interior.

The "Commonwealth" legal designation defines the Northern Mariana Islands as an organized jurisdiction that is unincorporated within the US national body-politic.[4] The Commonwealth Covenant is not organized under an Organic Act but instead organized vis-à-vis the Commonwealth

Covenant passed by the US Congress and authorized by President Gerald Ford. The Commonwealth Covenant was negotiated by the Mariana Political Status Commission, composed of representatives from the Northern Mariana and the US from 1972 to 1975. The Commonwealth Covenant was developed to replace the Trusteeship Agreement with a sovereign form of political relationship with the United States. The Northern Mariana negotiators wanted to define a distinctive relationship that afforded greater self-governance and to limit the federal government's reach. The Northern Marianas negotiated terms for a Constitution and full domestic self-governance, while offering the United States complete authority and responsibility for all foreign matters and military defense. The Northern Mariana people developed their own Constitution and the Commonwealth Covenant, which granted them complete autonomy for all domestic affairs under the lawful provisions of the Constitution.[5] The Commonwealth Covenant established a presidential representative democratic government with a Constitution. This hybrid system of self-government and political union with the United States is truly a distinctive relationship, as it was negotiated by CNMI representatives to strengthen the relationship between CNMI and the United States.

The Commonwealth Covenant went through a rigorous vetting and electoral ballot process. In 1975, the legislature of the Mariana Islands District of the UN Trust Territory of the Pacific Islands first passed it. Four months later, the Commonwealth Covenant was put up for a plebiscite vote, and 79 percent of all registered voters approved. President Ford signed Public Law 94-214, the Covenant to Establish a Commonwealth of the Northern Mariana Islands in Political Union with the United States of America, on March 24, 1976 (48 U.S.C. § 1801). On November 3, 1986, the UN terminated the Trusteeship Agreement between the Mariana Islands, and their people achieved their right of self-determination when the UN formally recognized the Commonwealth Covenant.

National Government

The Mariana Islands government operates according to its 1978 Constitution, which was modeled on the American structure and includes executive, legislative, and judicial branches. Under the Commonwealth Covenant, it adheres to the US Constitution, which prohibits all states, territories, and the Mariana Islands from entering into treaties with other countries. The Mariana Islands are prohibited from engaging in any bilateral or multi-lateral treaties under its political union with the United

States. The Mariana Islands are free to participate in international organizations to advance its development, but it cannot enter into any trade treaties under these organizational umbrellas. Typically, the US State Department has a representative at the international and regional organizations to negotiate on matters such as trade and defense.

Local Government

The Mariana Islands Constitution outlines the local government structure, which is led by mayors who represent the islands of north of Saipan, Aguigan, Tinian, and Rota (Constitution of Mariana Islands 1978, art. VI). The mayors sit on the Governor's Council to advise on domestic matters including local services, appropriations, budget, and the career service system and to act as the lead individuals in natural disaster emergencies in and throughout all islands. Powers are also given to the elected municipal councils in these islands.

Sources of Law: Customary Law and Western Law

The Mariana Islands have a Constitution, but the Commonwealth Covenant expressly includes specific provisions of the US Constitution, US treaties, pre-Commonwealth laws, and US laws reign supreme. The legal and political hybrid created under the Commonwealth Covenant is complicated but unquestionably benefits the Mariana Islands, which are tied to the United States but retain domestic sovereignty. For example, the Commonwealth Covenant expressly recognizes select sections of the US Constitution applicable to the Mariana Islands: it prohibits any denial of habeas corpus (right of individuals to know what they are being charged with by a judge or magistrate), affords US citizenship and the requisite full privileges and immunities including Bill of Rights freedoms, guarantees freedom from slavery, prevents the Mariana Islands Constitution from impeding any of the freedoms inherent in the US Constitution, and grants the right to vote. On the other hand, the Constitution of Northern Mariana Islands does not require indictments by grand jury or trial by jury. The Commonwealth Constitution enumerates rights, government and separation of powers, and other taxing powers like those found in continental states but also restricts the alienation of land.

Pre-Commonwealth laws from under the Trust Territory for the Mariana Islands district, if not inconsistent with the US Constitution,

Commonwealth Constitution, or treaties and laws of the United States, are still applicable to CNMI. There is no language in the CNMI Constitution that explicitly addresses custom or traditional law, and it is the responsibility of the Commonwealth Law Reform Commission to draft legislation for the Legislature where there is a gap. Traditional law is addressed in ad hoc fashion, with custom and tradition recognized in different jurisdictions, particularly in the case of family land. In the absence of customary law and written law, the rules of common law written by the American Law Institute are applied to the CNMI courts (Commonwealth of the Northern Marianas Code Tit. 7 § 3401).

Land Tenure and Governance

CNMI is the quintessential example of how hundreds of years of foreign occupation, domination, and control destroy indigenous land tenure. The Commonwealth Covenant and the local Constitution instituted a hard line on the issue of land. The privatization of land under waves of Spanish, German, and Japanese foreign colonizers eradicated the traditional Chamorro land holding system. Indigenous land holdings were eliminated, and large tracts of Chamorro lands were sold to non-Chamorros without consent or payment, which led to the eventual privatization of lands.

In the Islands, the local blood threshold requires an individual to be at least 25 percent descended from Northern Mariana Chamorro or Northern Mariana Carolinas descent to be considered a person of Northern Mariana ancestry (Constitution of Mariana Islands 1978, art. XII; see also *Warbol v. Villacrusis,* 958 F.2d 1450, 1462 (9th Cir. 1992)).[6] Like in American Sāmoa, land ownership is restricted to only Northern Mariana ancestry, which includes the conveyance of lands through sale, gift, or inheritance. A land commission creates plats, surveys, and determinations of title that influence decisions and registration of titles to land, and these documents go hand in hand with the Superior Court's certification of the 25 percent blood ancestry requirement.

The Constitution established the Mariana Public Land Corporation (PLC) to manage all public lands, which now account for at least 80 percent of all lands in the Mariana Islands (Constitution of Mariana Islands 1978, art. XI). A separate Trust handles all finances in relation to the management and operation of all public lands (Constitution of Mariana Islands 1978, art. XI).

Plausible Alternative Political and Legal Status

Following World War II, Pacific Islanders combatted colonization, war, assimilation, and foreign control and ownership of their government and native lands. Each island jurisdiction forged its own political framework to establish or reclaim self-government and sovereignty. In every transition from colonial entity to independent state, freely associated state, or commonwealth, negotiations revolved around the need to secure a future for the next generations of indigenous islanders. Future generations were the driving force behind the fight to stop the alienation of lands; by reclaiming control over their lands, indigenous people hoped to secure the culture and communal lands necessary to practice traditions. Stopping the alienation of lands meant stopping cultural death. Plausible alternative legal relationships with the United States are examined in this chapter, their experiences and roadmaps to self-determination offer hard-won lessons and insights for the indigenous people of American Sāmoa.

Status as a freely associated state, together with a Commonwealth Covenant, would provide American Sāmoa full sovereignty over domestic matters. Foreign trade and defense might still come under the US purview should these terms be mutually agreed upon. Palau and CNMI have had over ten years of self-government in distinct forms of political union with the United States, and American Sāmoa should consider the stark realities of these arrangements before proceeding down a similar political road.

Palau is realizing that the 50-year timeline of US federal assistance may have been too short. The United States entered the compact with Palau in 1994, and in 2009, during its first review of this political union, the US Congress determined that funding through the Trust for Palau needed to be decreased between FY 2012 to FY 2023. The US Congress required Palau to make meaningful economic reforms; if it did not, the US Congress would delay payments to the Trust, and after FY 2044 there would be no more direct US assistance or contributions to Palau (Loi 2011, testimony).

Citizenship also presents some significant complications. Under the COFA, Palau is sovereign and has its own citizenship. Under the Commonwealth Covenant, those living in CNMI are US citizens. Sāmoa is sovereign and not in any legal political union with the United States and has its own citizenship. It is doubtful that American Sāmoa would choose independence and have its own citizenship. If American Sāmoa wanted to negotiate a Commonwealth Covenant, would the political atmosphere embrace this type of change to its political union with the United States? Could individuals refuse to become US citizens? What does American Sāmoa have to gain and lose by negotiating a different type of political union with the United States? The advantages of a Commonwealth Covenant would include much more self-governance, negotiated sovereignty and freedom from the US federal laws over communal land tenure, freedom to enhance the protections of custom and traditions, and the ability to exercise the right to self-determination. Besides the citizenship considerations, the disadvantages include disruptions to direct and indirect financial assistance, contributions and grant-in-aid programs, and negative impacts on the Medicaid program which is currently 100 percent subsidized with no co-payments and deductibles, with all the population presumed eligible.[7] All the past Future Political Status Study Commissions have explicitly mentioned not wanting automatic US citizenship as it was granted to Guam through the Organic Act.

American Sāmoa is in a unique position to analyze and appreciate the negative impacts of the CNMI and Palau political and economic arrangements under the Freely Associated States and Commonwealth Covenants with the United States. Considering that under its present relationship, American Sāmoa is the only territory to receive appropriations and grants that comprise 63 percent of local government operations, health care is 100 percent subsidized, and communal lands and *mātai* system are protected under the local Constitution, changes to the present relationship should be undertaken only after careful analysis of the potential challenges contained in alternative political models ("Transforming the Economy" 1992).

Notes

1. *Tama'aiga* titles: *Malietoa*, *Tupua Tamasese*, *Mata'afa*, and *Tuimaleali'ifano*.
2. Freehold lands are not subject to the *pule* of the villages. The freehold landowners and their interests are represented in Parliament through these two "individual role" seats.
3. There are approximately 380 village councils throughout Sāmoa.
4. See Chap. 3 for distinctions between organized, unorganized, incorporated, and unincorporated US territories. CNMI are US citizens and are entitled to all the privileges and immunities that all citizens of the United States enjoy with the exception of voting for the President of the United States (every four years) and to US Congressional elections (Commonwealth Covenant art. III).

5. The Constitution of Northern Mariana Islands took effect in 1978.
6. The prohibition on the alienation of permanent and long-term interests in real property to persons other than those of Northern Mariana Islands descent was constitutional; in particular the opinion explains the application of constitutional principles must be designed "to incorporate the shared beliefs of diverse cultures…Its bold purpose was to protect minority rights," *Warbol v. Villacrusis*, 958 F.2d 1450 at 1392, 1462 (9th Cir. 1992).
7. The Medicaid program in American Sāmoa operates differently from the 50 states and District of Columbia; eligibility for Medicaid is not evaluated on an individual basis but eligibility is presumed. There are no TANF or SSI programs in American Sāmoa. Every year the percentage of the population below 200 percent of the poverty level is calculated and approved by Centers for Medicaid and Medicare Services (CMS); CMS pays expenditures for Medicaid based on the approved calculations.

References

Warbol v. Villacrusis, 958 F.2d 1450, 1462 (9th Cir. 1992).
48 U.S.C. § 1801.
1947 United Nations Trusteeship art.3.
Alienation of Freehold Land Act 1972 §2.
Commonwealth of the Northern Marianas Code Tit. 7 § 3401.
Compact of Free Association (COFA), P.L. 99-658.
Constitution of Independent State of Sāmoa art. IV, C(1)(c).
Constitution of Independent State of Sāmoa arts. 101, 102.
Constitution of Mariana Islands 1978, art. VI.
Constitution of Mariana Islands 1978, art. XI.
Constitution of Mariana Islands 1978, art. XII.
Constitution of Palau art. II.
Constitution of Palau art. IX.
Palau National Code Title I, §302.
Palau National Code Title 39.
Sāmoa Land and Titles Act 1981.
Sāmoa Land Titles Registration Act 2008.
Sui O Le Malo Act 1978.
American Samoa Economic Advisory Committee. 1992. *Transforming the Economy of American Samoa: A Report to the President of the United States through the Secretary of the Department of Interior*, vol. 2.
Cortes, Antonio. 1987. "Land in Trust: The Invasion of Palau's Land-Tenure Customs by American Law." *Asian-Pacific Law & Policy Journal* 14 (3): 167–240.

Loi, James. 2011. Testimony before the House Foreign Affairs Committee, Subcommittee on Asia and the Pacific. *Compact of Free Association of Palau: Assessing the 15-Year Review*. November 30. http://www.state.gov/p/eap/rls/rm/2011/11/177965.htm.

Meller, Norman. 2000. Indigenous Self Determination and Its Implementation. *Pacific Studies* 23 (1/2): 1.

Sāmoa Bureau of Statistics. 2011. Report. Population and Housing Census.

US Citizenship and Immigration Services. *US Immigration Law in the Commonwealth of the Northern Mariana Islands (CNMI)*. Website Accessed 1 January 2016.

U.S. Citizenship and Immigration Services. *Federated States of Micronesia, Republic of the Marshall Islands, and Palau*. Website Accessed 1 January 2016.

US Government Accountability Office GAO-12-798T. 2012. Report. Compact of Free Association: Proposed U.S. Assistance to Palau through Fiscal Year 2024.

United Nations Charter chapt. XII, art. 77.

CHAPTER 10

Conclusion

I'a ulu'ulu Mata-Folau

The history of American Sāmoa is an intricate and intriguing history as an unincorporated and unorganized territory. Over the first 50 years of US Naval oversight over the territory, American Sāmoans displayed outward symbols of Americanness proscribed by the Naval Administration, thus facilitating their acceptance into the American body-politic. Many American conservative traditionalists were concerned about the introduction of foreign culture, language, and geographic remoteness and worried about the level of political acquiescence that would be required. A concrete political and legal relationship was required to delineate what and how American Sāmoa was to operate within this ambiguous territorial relationship.

The absolute oversight by the Naval Administration and changes it implemented in customary land tenure suggest the federal-territorial experience was not just about geopolitical aggrandizement or the opportunity to enlarge the American family. Instead, American Sāmoa was a vehicle of engagement in the wider world beyond continental America. Without an Organic Act or legal instrument to guide the Navy in governing this unincorporated and unorganized territory, which was ceded to the United States through two Deeds of Cession, the Navy became the executive, legislative, and judicial overseer. This form of governance was undemocratic and unchecked; there was too much power vested in the

Sāmoan proverb, it means to have a vision while on a journey.

L.-N. Memea Kruse, *The Pacific Insular Case of American Sāmoa*,
https://doi.org/10.1007/978-3-319-69971-4_10

Commandant-Governor. As Navy Captain Stephen V. Graham, 18th Governor of American Sāmoa, wrote in the *Honolulu Star-Bulletin* after two years serving in the territory, "I also felt that the governor as the sole legislative branch of the government was clothed with too much power under any form of government and more particularly under an American government" (Graham 1929, p. 4). California judge C.S. Hannum protested to President Warren Harding over the undemocratic rule in American Sāmoa in 1925, "The Naval governor has been permitted an absolute dictatorship. He has ordered, and from this order the civilian population has no redress..." (Hannum 1925, letter).

The Navy introduced adverse land possession as a method for determining land rights and ownership according to western standards. In one of the first land cases heard by the High Court in the early 1900s, the oral tradition of claiming ownership of communal lands was determined to be inadequate by western standards. "In this world of uncertainty," the Court wrote, "the gradual progress of civilization tends to eliminate uncertainties, and one of the blessings of civilization is stability of land titles" (*Talala v. Logo*, 1 A.S.R. 166, 189 (1907)). The Navy was promoting democracy and acceptable national idealism when it ruled that oral tradition without surveys or written land titles was discredited as uncivilized and therefore undemocratic. Actual, hostile, open, notorious, exclusive, and continuous possession of land was defined by the Navy as the "method of acquisition of title by possession" to claim real property title (*Talo v. Poi*, 2 A.S.R. 9, 11–12 (1938)). Oral tradition as testimony to evidence claim of customary land rights was only credible within specific parameters, which then military jurists consistently curtailed and limited. Virgin communal lands were legally reconstructed into unowned property, thereby dispossessing the village of ownership rights.

Through the Navy's adjudication of land disputes, it supported conceptions of property based on the ideologies of social justice expressed in English common law—in other words, western notions of law and society favoring the rights of individuals over the rights of groups. Professor M.D. Olson writes:

> The Courts, which tended not to reflect upon the inconsistencies, tended to re-interpret as 'Samoan custom' the conceptions of land rights which the colonial state's civilizing influence attempted to effect, promoting, in the process, a more general acceptance of the concepts within Samoan societies. (Olson 2000, p. 34)

Once Sāmoans realized that the High Court recognized and conferred rights on individuals, claims of individualized land through adverse possession began to surface. This was the window that opened up individually owned land rights—a land tenure classification that did not exist before 1900. Today, individually owned lands compose 26 percent of land ownership in American Sāmoa. The abject neglect the Court paid to the preservation of custom and customary lands when it appropriated and applied English common law, and particularly adverse land possession concepts, has led to what he describes as the "derogation of Sāmoan custom" (*Re: In the matter of the high chief title "Mauga,"* 4 A.S.R. 132 (1974)).

Some of the historical texts reveal that neither the Navy nor Congress conspired to abolish Sāmoan indigenous culture or destroy the communal land tenure when the islands were ceded to the United States. Arguably, then, from the beginning there was bureaucratic misgiving by the Navy to develop the Tutuila Naval Station and to administer American Sāmoa; there was no vision, direction, guidance, funding, and integrated purpose aligned with the military mandates for American Sāmoa. The introduction of adverse possession rights apportioned communal tracts of land. The High Court redefined bush lands as belonging to no one. Meaning, all lands unoccupied and uncultivated belonged to no one and not under the *fa'amātai* authority. When interpreted in the historical context of the broader scheme of American expansionist strategies during the nineteenth century, this evolution reveals a great deal about American Sāmoa's struggles within the federal-territorial status, and, more broadly, exposes the negotiations of American cultural and political identity in wider global contexts.

I've demonstrated the undercurrents of the indeterminate relationship between the United States and American Sāmoa and how these undercurrents define the federal-territorial experience. I have also elucidated how these complexities led to the splitting of communal lands by the Navy. Individualized land rights confer security of tenure against the *āiga* members. The traditional Sāmoan social norms based on reciprocity and rights and obligations of kin have changed due to the creation of individualized land tenure from adverse possession. At this present time, the practice of traditional Sāmoan customs within a global market demands land tenure modification to the existing structure. Unless the *Fono* stops the individualization of land that removes land from customary stewardship and under the *fa'amātai*, a balance of cultural protections and economic growth could be found through codifying individual lands similar to the classification of freehold lands. This would allow the owner to freely transfer land (with or without American Sāmoan ancestry). American Sāmoa could also approach this issue with a firm hand and move for the dissolution of individual land ownership through law, referendum by vote through legislation, or amendment to the Constitution.

Perhaps, this is the time to legislate this hybrid lifestyle into the land tenure classification system by protecting virgin and customary lands from further alienation while also allowing freehold and individual lands to be freely transferable. Under this change, only these specific lands could be used as acceptable security to lending institutions. In Independent State of Sāmoa, they amended the Limitation Amendment Act 1975 in 2012 and completely dissolved adverse possession rights (Limitation Act of Sāmoa 1975, Part I (9)).[1] Parliament recognized that adverse possession claims were an unfair practice that limited the right of a dispossessed owner.

American Sāmoa, after looking at the process and results of changes in political status of other Insular Areas, may seek alternative political and legal arrangements that can strengthen the ability to further protect the *fa'amātai* and communal land tenure systems, thus preserving Sāmoan culture and identity. There is relatively little scholarship on Sāmoan culture and the impacts that individually owned land has wrought upon it and upon communal land tenure. My sincere hope is that this book will incite more examination and conversation in this area of American Sāmoan customary land and law.

Notes

1. Actions to recover land or register title—(1) Subject to section 3(1) of the Limitation Amendment Act 2012 and to this part, from January 26, 2012: (1) no right, title or interest in or to land adverse to or in derogation of the title of the registered owner shall be acquired by any length of possession by virtue of any adverse possession relating to real property; and (2) no right, title or interest in or to land adverse to or in derogation of the title of the registered owner shall be registered by virtue of a claim to title by adverse possession; and (3) no title of any such registered owner shall be extinguished by the operation of any statute of limitation. (2) Subject to section 3(1) of the Limitation Amendment Act 2012 and to this part, from January 26, 2012: (1) no right, title or interest in or to land shall be acquired by adverse possession; and (2) no right, title or interest in or to land shall be registered by virtue of a claim to title by adverse possession; and (3) no party shall raise adverse possession to defend or resist any claim by a registered owner to—(a) recover land; or (b) evict a party; or (c) redefine boundaries of land.

References

Re: In the matter of the high chief title "Mauga", 4 A.S.R. 132 (1974).

Talala v. Logo, 1 A.S.R. 166, 189 (1907).

Talo v. Poi, 2 A.S.R. 9, 11–12 (1938).

Limitation Act of Sāmoa 1975, Part I (9).

Graham, Stephen V. 1929. "Ex-Governor of Samoa Says Navy Rule Is Best." *Honolulu Star Bulletin*, 4. August 16.

Hannum, C.S. 1925. C.S. Hannum Letter to President Warren Harding. December 10.

Olson, M.D. 2000. "Articulating Custom: Politics and Poetics of Social Transformations in Samoa." *Journal of Legal Pluralism* 32 (45): 34.

Glossary of Sāmoan Words

āiga Family, kin.

āiga potopoto Extended family, kin; also, collective term for all the members of a lineage who have the right to be present at, and to take part in, the election of a new *mātai*.

'aufono Council.

Aufono o Ali'i Council of Chiefs.

'aumaga Untitled men.

'aualuma Girls and young women.

fa'asāmoa Customs and ways of behaving as well as words of deference and respect which every Sāmoan must practice each day.

fa'alavelave Cultural and family-related events that require family members to contribute money and/or commodity items (fine mats) for weddings, funerals, *mātai* titles, and church activities, as well as providing financial assistance for basic family needs.

fa'amātai Complex configuration of *mātai* titles, all ordered relative to each other. *Mātai* titles are based upon kinship relations, mythology, and genealogical history but are also influenced by one's ability to garner loyalty and support within the *āiga* and *āiga potopoto* structure. Each nuclear household has a *mātai* title holder in traditional Sāmoan society and on communal lands within the village. Within the village there is a hierarchy of *mātai* title holders and each *mātai* title is ranked relative to the others.

Fa'asuaga Paramount Chief in American Sāmoa.

Faipule Lower House of Legislature.

L.-N. Memea Kruse, *The Pacific Insular Case of American Sāmoa*,
https://doi.org/10.1007/978-3-319-69971-4

faletalimālo Customary structures reserved for *mātai*.
fono Meeting or council.
Fono Aoao Faitulafono National Legislative Assembly.
itūmālō District.
malae Open land reserved for greeting visitors, playing sports, and village gatherings.
malae-fono Meeting grounds.
malaga Ceremonial visit paid according to Sāmoan custom; visiting guests.
mālō National government.
mātai Titled head of a Sāmoan extended family; also, the steward representing a family in communal land matters and before the local political councils (village council), as well as between families in discussions and disputes for possible arbitration and resolution.
nu'u Village.
papālagi White foreigners.
poumuli tree Durable tree used as poles for traditional houses and cooking houses.
pule Power or authority.
pulenu'u Liaisons between the customary Sāmoan system of government and the central government.
sā Taboo, forbidden.
Sa'o Senior *mātai* title holder (out of several in a lineage).
suli moni Individual connected through blood descent.
suli sili Individual from different family who nonetheless lives with and renders service to Sa'o.
suli fa'i Individual who is an adopted heir, not of blood descent, also considered to have rendered service to Sa'o.
ta'amū Variety of giant taro.
Tama'āiga Royal title.
taeao History.
tagata mālo Guest.
Ta'imua House of High Chiefs.
tautua Service. For untitled individuals, service to *mātai*; service as a means to gain authority as a *mātai*; service as *mātai* to family and extended family as part of role and responsibility.
Tulafale mātai Orator, talking chief.

Index[1]

[1] Note: Page numbers followed by "n" refers to notes.

L.-N. Memea Kruse, *The Pacific Insular Case of American Sāmoa*,
https://doi.org/10.1007/978-3-319-69971-4

CPSIA information can be obtained
at www.ICGtesting.com
Printed in the USA
LVHW081714140620
657944LV00010B/232